MW01514299

Suggested Preparation for Careers in Security/Loss Prevention

Second Edition

John Chuvala III

Robert James Fischer

Western Illinois University

KENDALL/HUNT PUBLISHING COMPANY
4050 Westmark Drive   Dubuque, Iowa 52002

DEDICATION

In memory of my father and mother, John and
Evelyn Chuvala. Thanks for everything.

John Chuvala III

To my wife Kathy and my many friends who
have contributed to the advance of loss prevention
literature and theory.

Robert James Fischer

Contents

PREFACE AND ACKNOWLEDGMENTS

As students, teachers, and practitioners in the field of security/loss prevention, we have often been frustrated in locating a book which discusses the basic disciplines or specific course work which is necessary for a person who wishes to pursue a career in the field. While the work by the American Society for Industrial Security (ASIS) provided guidelines for the establishment of academic programs, serious discussion regarding various courses were only summarized by the ASIS Standing Committee on Academic Programs in Colleges and Universities in the following statement:

... an academic background in security combines well with other majors to make the graduate even more attractive to potential employers. Security students should also consider studying computer science, electronics, business management. law, police science, personnel, and information management.

Building on this basic statement we have developed a book of readings gathered from recognized leaders, both practitioners and academicians (from both security and other fields). These contributing authors are the textbook. They have their own unique way of presenting what they believe to be the key to success given their own specialization and background. The common thread which runs through all the chapters is the need for security/loss prevention personnel to have a broad understanding of various disciplines and specific skills for certain chosen specialties. As summarized in Chapter 1, "Career Opportunities in Loss Prevention," the future is bright for students seeking careers in this growing field.

It should not be assumed that all subjects discussed in this book by various authors should be attempted by students. Rather, it is likely that as students begin to focus on a specific area of loss prevention, they will be able to utilize the wisdom of our contributing authors in picking minor areas and elective courses. The contributing authors are experts within their areas whether attorneys, sociologists, security managers or investigators. However, this book does focus on specific skills which students should consider: communication, management and law. Other subject areas such as fire, computer security, etc. will depend on the student's interests.

The editors would like to thank all the contributing authors for their willingness to give personal time to this project. Most have very heavy work commitments and we greatly appreciate their willingness to work with us and meet deadlines. We would also like to express our thanks to our original production staff, Raylene Prentice and Barbara Ritchey. Without their skills this book would still be in draft form. We also thank Kandy Enright, who has spent hours editing the current manuscript. Finally, we thank the publisher for his encouragement and support throughout the duration of this project.

The editors,

John Chuvala, III & Robert James Fischer

INTRODUCTION

This book of readings was developed to serve primarily as a supplement to various introductory security textbooks. The articles provide the reader with insight into the vast interdisciplinary nature of the security field. The chapters which follow will provide guidance to any student who may need help in choosing a career or who wants to know what courses to study to be able to gain a competitive edge in the security field.

The chapters are organized into two parts. Part I, "Careers in Security/Loss Prevention and Basic Security Career Skills," discusses career options in general and provides specific discussion of an investigative career. In addition, the other chapters in Part I are designed to provide loss prevention/security students with an understanding of the basic disciplines necessary in developing a successful career in the field. These areas include communications skills, the importance of understanding people (sociological knowledge), legal issues, and the importance of management skills.

Part II, "Security Specialties," presents a variety of chapters written by experts in specific areas of the loss prevention/security field. These include: personnel management, technology, computer security. fire science and emergency procedures, disaster planning, risk management, and insurance. The study of security/loss prevention is an area where opportunities are plentiful for the person who is willing to pursue certain basic areas of study.

CHAPTER 1

CAREER OPPORTUNITIES
IN LOSS PREVENTION

Robert James Fischer, Ph.D.
Director, Illinois Law Enforcement Executive Institute

Today security is a major management function in American business. Where, almost unheard of 30 or even 20 years ago, there are now vice presidents of loss prevention reporting directly to the presidents of many companies and having the same impact on management decisions as do, for example, the vice presidents of operations or distribution.

Career opportunities in different areas of business, industry, and government security vary; the perceived need for an integral and integrated security function in the management of the widest variety of enterprises can be anticipated as becoming the norm in the near future.

Factors Increasing
Security Opportunities

Among the factors that tend to create inviting career paths in security, none is more significant than the explosive growth of the protection function. The number of personnel engaged in private security will double between 1980 and 2000 to more than 1.8 million persons. Various studies place the growth rate generally for security products and services at 12 percent to 15 percent annually, and there is no sign of slowing. Rapid advances in electronic technology create new opportunities almost daily (Cunningham, Strauchs and Van Meter, 1990).

Other positive considerations for the future of not only jobs in security but also the changes and requirements for individual advancement or growth within the career field include the following:

- The increasing professionalism of security is reflected in higher standards of educational criteria and experience and correspondingly higher salaries, especially at management levels.

- The rapid growth of the loss-prevention function has created a shortage of qualified personnel with management potential, meaning less competition and greater opportunities for advancement for those who are qualified.

- The shift in emphasis to programs of prevention and service rather than of control or law enforcement has broadened the security function within the typical organization.

- The presence of both two- and four-year degree programs as well as master's-level study in criminal justice and/or security at the college level is creating a new awareness of a rising generation of trained security personnel at the corporate management level. Many companies, especially larger corporations, are actively emphasizing the degree approach in hiring.

As in many other areas of a society that is belatedly recognizing the needs and the potential contributions of women, blacks, and other minorities, opportunities for these groups are particularly good. *Hallcrest II* points out the scarcity of good demographic information on personnel employed in the security field. Yet if the Hallcrest II study of St. Louis is any indication, the number of women in private security has doubled within the last 15 years. The employment of minorities, particularly blacks, has remained at about 50 percent (Cunningham, et al).

The Security/
Loss-Prevention Occupation

No matter whether you recognize the protection function by titles such as loss prevention, security administration, or industrial security, the basic function of modern security remains the same. Security helps prevent losses. Losses from crime have continued to increase despite the decline in criminal behavior reported through the National Crime Survey (NCS) and the Uniform Crime Reports (UCR). For every product manufactured, someone is waiting to make an illegal profit by stealing or through manipulation of processes and records. For every security device installed, someone is determined to find a method to defeat it. Steven C. Kaverman, CPP (Certified Protection Professional), asserts that the dynamic trends of the 1990s will affect our businesses in the year 2000 and beyond. "Team management concepts, a changing work force, and educational demands are three issues that will pose a universal challenge to the flexibility of security professionals and corporate executives at every level." (1990) Much like law enforcement, security is basically a recession-proof occupation, particularly at line (guard) levels. The need for educated and trained security officers and administrators is increasing with the need to counteract terrorism, computer crime, embezzlement, employee theft, drugs and violence in the workplace, fraud, and shoplifting. The U.S. Department of Labor has identified security as one of the fastest-growing fields of employment. Estimates indicate that for every person hired in public law enforcement, three are hired in private security. *Hallcrest II* predicts that this trend will continue through the year 2000.

Security professionals are hired by almost all kinds of organizations at all levels-line; lower, middle, and upper management; corporate; and so on. Among organizations that have security operations are banks, colleges, government agencies, hospitals, public utilities, restaurants, hotels, retail stores, insurance companies, museums, mining firms, oil companies, supermarkets, telecommunications companies, transportation companies, and office buildings. Within each of these broad areas, security personnel perform many different functions, including personnel protection, computer security, coupon security, disaster management, crime prevention, proprietary information security, white-collar crime investigations, counterterrorism security, guard force management, investigations, physical security, crisis management, plant security, privacy and information management, fire prevention and safety, and drug abuse prevention and control.

The American Society for Industrial Security (ASIS) Committee on Academic Programs suggests that students seeking careers in security should pursue course work in security, computer science, electronics, business management, law, police science, personnel, and information management (ASIS Foundation). This theme is supported throughout the following chapters. Building on the ASIS committee statements, the editors developed a book of readings that have a common thread: the need for security/loss-prevention personnel to have a broad understanding of various disciplines and specific skills for certain specialties. The editors suggest that specific skills are needed for all students of security-communication, management, and law. Other subject areas, such as fire and computer security, will depend on the student's interests.

Security Manager

Salaries of security directors with policy making authority average $67,617 per year according to a 1996 survey conducted by Langer and Associates. Salaries for those with only three or four years of experience average $53,045, while salaries for those with 25 or more years average $78,363. This is an increase of 7.2 percent over the 1994 figures. The average 1996 security executive has 1-5 or more years of experience and a graduate degree (M.S. or Ph.D.), has a CPP certification, and is involved with both the Department of Defense and the Department of Energy. While the average salary is $67,616, many security directors make over $250,000 per year (Langer, 1996; 76). Figure 1.1 provides additional information on salaries.

Bodyguard

There were 322 terrorist incidents throughout the world in 1995. With the danger of kidnapping and threats from other areas (including disgruntled employees) the demand for executive protection specialists, or bodyguards, is increasing (Leader, 1997; 34).

According to John Viggiano of Dignitary Protection and Investigative Services, New York, "Television makes it look like [bodyguards] have to be 6'3" with blond hair, blue eyes, and a California tan. That is nonsense. What they need is common sense, the ability to pay attention to detail, and patience."(Mack, 1984; 126) Bodyguards should also know about laws and customs in different places (countries, states, cities) where they might be living or traveling with their principals. In a field once dominated by men, women are becoming more prominent as protection specialists. Most employers of executive protection specialists want a person who can fit into the executive's work and play schedule.

Figure 1.1
Average Annual Mean Income of Security Directors

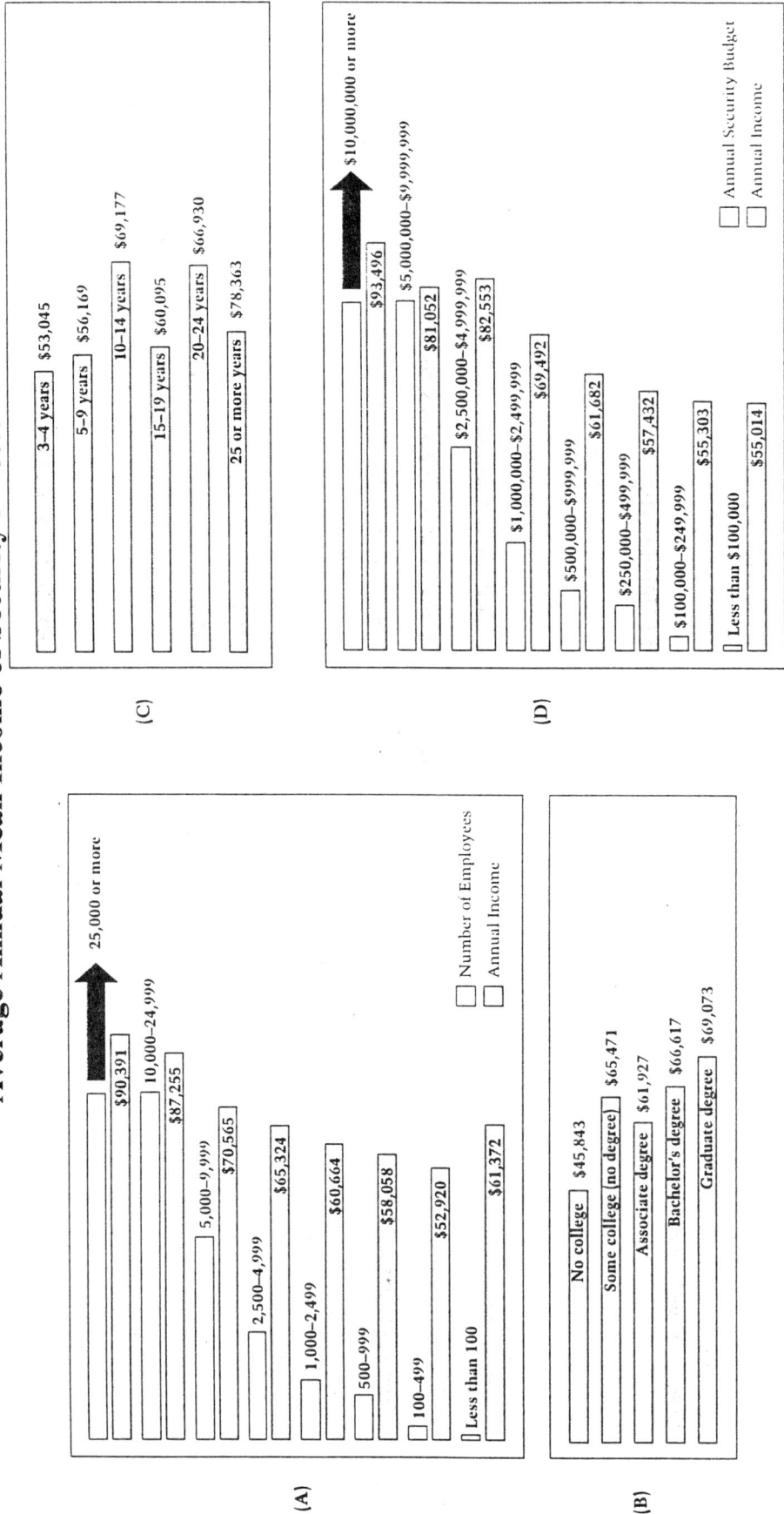

(C)

- 3–4 years $53,045
- 5–9 years $56,169
- 10–14 years $69,177
- 15–19 years $60,095
- 20–24 years $66,930
- 25 or more years $78,363

(D)

- $10,000,000 or more
- $5,000,000–$9,999,999 $93,496
- $2,500,000–$4,999,999 $81,052
- $1,000,000–$2,499,999 $82,553
- $500,000–$999,999 $69,492
- $250,000–$499,999 $61,682
- $100,000–$249,999 $57,432
- Less than $100,000 $55,303
- $55,014

☐ Annual Security Budget
☐ Annual Income

(A)

- 25,000 or more
- 10,000–24,999 $90,391
- 5,000–9,999 $87,255
- 2,500–4,999 $70,565
- 1,000–2,499 $65,324
- 500–999 $60,664
- 100–499 $58,058
- Less than 100 $52,920
- $61,372

☐ Number of Employees
☐ Annual Income

(B)

- No college $45,843
- Some college (no degree) $65,471
- Associate degree $61,927
- Bachelor's degree $66,617
- Graduate degree $69,073

Figure 1.1 Average mean annual income of security directors by A) size of organization, B) level of education, C) length of experience, and total annual security budget. Modified from Steven Langer, "The Wages of Security." Reprinted from the August 1996 issue of Security Management, American Society for Industrial Security, 1655 North Fort Myer Drive, Suite

4

Bodyguard schools are now becoming prominent and many of the students are former law enforcement or military personnel. Skills taught include use of weapons and hand-to-hand combat. In addition, schools might also prepare the specialists with skills in protocol, dress, and specialized knowledge of alarm systems and closed-circuit TV (CCTV). While the salaries and benefits are generally excellent, burnout is high. Long hours and time spent away from friends and family eventually take their toll.

Private Investigators

In general, private investigators (PIs) are involved in locating missing persons, obtaining confidential information, and solving crimes. Many PIs work for businesses and lawyers whereas others work independently. Independent offices may be only one-person operations or may employ several operatives or contract work to part-time investigators. These independent investigators charge from $35 to over $150 per hour. Long days and seven-day workweeks are the norm when a PI is on a case.

Good PIs develop skills that include the ability to conduct good surveillance and background checks. Some cases involve undercover investigations and require a complete understanding of a sometimes dangerous assignment, including developing a cover and dealing with people who must not know who you are. The private investigation business requires the investigator to learn the law and interviewing and investigative techniques. The best PIs also possess good verbal and written skills as well as analytical skills. Attendance at or membership in the National Association of Legal Investigators is an excellent aid to improving basic skills. Generally speaking, the outlook for jobs in this area is good. According to the bureau, the market is stable and good in all states.

A person interested in this field should consult individual state laws, which vary greatly, to determine what criteria must be met for licensing. Criteria vary from virtually none to extensive experience, completion of a written and/or oral examination, and interview by a state board.

Consultants

Security consultants are the specialists of the field. They generally operate as sole proprietors of a business that sells specific security expertise. Some security consultants charge more than $100 per hour and bill over $200,000 annually. Security consultants provide advice for a fee. They do not work for specific equipment companies or firms. Advice commonly purchased from the consultant consists of information from three general areas:

1. Number, quantity, and use of security personnel
2. Direction and content of security policies and procedures
3. Alternatives in security hardware

Consultants also offer training seminars on specific problem areas, for example, executive protection and disaster planning.

Security consultants are generally people who have paid their dues working in investigation or security management. Many have published articles and books. Today the completion of a Ph.D. is helpful since the title "Doctor" carries added weight if the consultant is called to testify in court. As civil litigation increases, the demand for "security experts" who can testify as credible witnesses also increases.

Opportunities in Industry

Typically the greatest opportunities in industrial security exist in larger companies that employ proprietary security forces. The career oriented person with a certificate or degree in a recognized security or criminal justice program is actively recruited by many firms.

However, the trend toward hybrid security operations has reduced the demand for proprietary security officers in many companies. The largest employers, such as General Motors, John Deere, and Caterpillar, are making a transition to a system of contract officers with proprietary oversight. In addition these industrial giants have been actively installing state-of-the-art technology that has changed the need for security officers.

Despite this reduction in demand, the security director at one major manufacturing facility with a highly progressive security program reports being interested in hiring only those applicants with at least a B.S. in security from a recognized security or criminal justice program.

Opportunities in Retail

The retail field provides a diversity of job opportunities in security, from the entry-level position of the uniformed security officer (or blazer-jacketed "host") to the shoplifting investigator. Positions are available both with retail stores, chains and with security service companies, which provide such services as undercover and shopping investigations. There are many openings for those without experience but with education, ambition, and aptitude they may become successful in retail security. Many companies today provide their own training for shoppers and other investigators even though the employees have no investigative experience. Alertness, resourcefulness, courage, and self-assurance are often more important than specific experience.

There are many different types of operations in the retail industry. Security has had its impact in virtually every operation-from the discount store through the department store to the supermarket. The recognition of the importance of inventory shrinkage to the company's profit picture and the necessity for loss prevention is, or soon will be, almost universal. Those companies that do not accept this necessity, in the words of one ranking retail executive, "simply will not remain in business."

The entry-level position in one company includes many students recruited from criminal justice and security programs as well as sales personnel crossing over to security. Many of these employees work part-time while they are going to school.

Opportunities in Health Care

Hospital security officers make up the vast majority of persons employed in hospital security. According to Russell Colling, a nationally known health care security authority and author of *Hospital Security*, the officer who prepares for advancement (through a combination of education beyond high school and field experience) can look to numerous supervisory, investigative, training, fire prevention, and safety positions in the field (1982).

Hospital security officers generally earn more than do their counterparts in other industries because of the variety of duties requiring a higher-than average amount of training. The officer must also be able to interact effectively with the medical community as well as with patients and visitors under conditions of frequent stress. Salaries, however, do vary by location.

Security director positions generally require at least four years of college preparation and considerable field experience. Like so many other areas of security, as Colling observes, hospital security is just coming into its own.

Airport and Airline Security

The airport and airline security field at the level above the line security officer is one that has been dominated by former law enforcement personnel, particularly former special agents of the FBI. The security directors of many major airlines are former FBI agents, and this is also true of many investigators.

This situation is not unique to airlines, of course. Former agents of the bureau can be found in a great many corporate security jobs in U.S. business and industry. Both the experience and the qualifications required by the FBI have generally been highly regarded in the private sector. The ambitious, career-minded security aspirant could do far worse than consider a period of service in the FBI as a springboard to a promising position in industry, including the airline industry.

Qualifications are high. Almost all employees in this field have college degrees. Many have law degrees and five or more years of FBI experience.

In airport security, a wide variety of entry-level positions exists for the line security officer, especially at major airports. Here again the field is relatively new, mushrooming especially since the hijacking scares that began in the late 1960s and continue today, even with increased security standards. It seems clear that, with mandated security requirements including physical security and access controls, baggage screening, 100 percent screening of air passengers and carry-on luggage, cargo security, and other controls, the demand for personnel to fill these needs will continue to rise.

Hotel Security

The hotel and motel industry has been characterized in the past by serious neglect of many security responsibilities, an attitude that has slowly been changing in spite of a number of very large awards by the courts in recent years against hotels or motels charged with negligent security, particularly in the area of protecting guests. This neglect, however, coupled with court-mandated responsibility, has created opportunity for security professionals

In the words of Walter J. Buzby, coauthor of *Hotel and Motel Security Management*, "[o]pportunities in the hotel industry exist in great numbers both for 'on-the-site' positions and at the corporate home office level." (1976) Except at the corporate level or the management level in large hotels, however, the salary range is relatively low in relation to the security industry as a whole. On the other side of the coin, the entry level for the person with any combination of hotel experience and security education or experience can be quite good, with clear opportunities for advancement.

In a related area, the future of security in high-rise apartment buildings and housing complexes offers great potential for the security professional because of the growing emphasis on the concept of total environmental protection and the threat of civil suits by residents or guests who are victimized on building property.

Campus Security

John W. Powell, nationally known campus security consultant and former security director at Yale University, observes that the rapid progress of campus security during the past 25 years has created excellent opportunities for career positions in the field. Openings in many progressive and professional campus departments provide not only challenge but also good salaries and fringe benefits as well as chances for advancement. Such departments are looking for the young, career-minded individual, with particular interest in those enrolled in, or graduates of, a criminal justice degree program. Interestingly, unlike many areas of modern security, campus security has generally evolved from a low-visibility operation to a highly visible, police-oriented image in response to rising crime problems on campuses.

A good-sized department will include line officers, field supervisors, shift commanders, a coordinator of line operations and a director. Many departments also have specialized positions such as investigator and training officer. Salaries vary from department to department, and from one area of the country to another.

Banking Security

Banks must comply with minimum federal regulations on security, as promulgated in the Bank Protection Act of 1968. The act mandates that there must be a security manager. Banks comply with this requirement in a variety of ways. Small operations often delegate security responsibilities to one of the senior bank officers. Larger banks, however, hire security managers who often are former FBI agents with an understanding of federal regulations regarding currency and fraud. There is a heavy reliance on electronic technology and physical security rather than on large staffs.

The bank guard may become a casualty of technological advances as many banks are finding it more cost-effective to eliminate guards in favor of physical security improvements.

Security Services

In general, security personnel at the lower operational levels earn less in contract security organizations than they do in proprietary guard forces. This is not necessarily true for investigators and other personnel at higher levels.

In the words of Saul Astor, president of Management Safeguards, Inc., "Young people should seek opportunities in security service organizations since the growth of security services has been meteoric and there is no leveling off in sight. The demand for good executives is insatiable. Very high salaries are being paid by security service organizations to the young newcomers" (1978).

Because the good loss-prevention or security executive is much less a policeman than a systems expert, auditor, and teacher, Astor recommends broad-based education and experience in such areas as accounting, industrial engineering, management, personnel, law, statistics, labor relations, and report writing.

On another level, the doubling of the number of security firms in less than a decade reflects the demand for technically qualified individuals capable of providing specialized security services ranging from alarm sales, installation, and service, to alarm systems consulting. Continuing changes in the application of security hardware and systems will bring an increasing demand for the services of those who can advise users on their selection and implementation.

Locksmithing

This is a classic profession requiring a lengthy apprenticeship. Locksmiths in the United States sell, install, and repair locking devices, safes, and vaults. Some also sell and install various alarm and electronic access-control systems (Cunningham, et al; 130). Positions are available in shops, where apprentice locksmiths spend their time learning the trade under a master craftsperson. Much of the work is done on an emergency basis, thus the hours are often long and irregular. The best jobs involve keying new facilities or rekeying older structures such as office buildings and motels.

Technology Experts

With the growing use of electronics in security, the demand for professionals who understand the applications of alarm technology, CCTV, and other high-tech applications within security is growing. Alarm installation is an excellent skill to learn. While most positions in this business are through distributors and contract security services, there is a trend toward proprietary positions. Certification for this area of study is available through the National Alarm Association of America (NAAA) (Keller, 1998).

Computer Security

This is an important example of the new frontiers opening in the loss-prevention field in response to social and technological changes. John Carroll, a leading computer scientist, security consultant, and author of *Computer Security,* calls for "a blend of education and experience in computer science and security (1987).

Today virtually all organizations have computers that need protection. In addition, many firms generate information, customer lists, research projects, and so on from these computer operations that also need protection. Table 1.1 lists some opportunities in computer security.

Conclusion

Although salary scales and security applications vary in different parts of the country as well as within the different areas of business and industry-or even within the same type of business or industry; it is nevertheless possible to perceive the coming of age of security throughout the 1990s and into the twenty-first century.

The aging, poorly trained, and underpaid guard portrayed by the 1968 Rand report is an exception today as observed by the 1990 *Hallcrest II* report. The latter report notes that today's guard is younger (average age is 35 compared to 42 in 1975), better paid, and better trained than was the case at the beginning of 1970. The guard is also just as likely to be black as white, and nearly 1 out of 10 guards is a black woman. The number of women in private security has doubled every 15 years. Educational levels are up from an average of 11 years of formal education in 1975 to over 85 percent having 12 or more years in 1989 (Cunningham, et al: 138-39).

Still, more universally accepted standards of training and applicant screening and higher wage scales are needed. The opportunity for vertical movement within the security structure must be both present and perceived. But even in these areas there are encouraging signs.

The use of outside investigators and security consultants will increase as security functions become more specialized. According to *Security,* the trend for the year 2000 will be toward hiring security services and consultants and keeping specialized proprietary staff at lower numbers (1989; 4).

Table 1.1 Opportunities in Computer Security

Title	Employer	Duties	Sources	Education
EDP security coordinator (administrator)	EDP centers	Works with conventional security forces, representatives of computer manufacturers and software houses, and local systems programmers to implement and maintain computer security systems.	Programmers or systems analysts with training in security.	Combination of education and experience in EDP equivalent to an M.S. in computer science (for example, two years' community college and six years' progressive experience in general EDP, or three years' community college and four years' experience, or B.S. in computer science and two years' experience), and part-time or full-time training in computer security—30 classroom hours with appropriate preparation and practicum.
EDP security analyst	Government, large-user companies	Prescribes, reviews and evaluates computer systems. Conducts security inspections, surveys, and threat evaluations.	EDP security coordinators or junior security analysts with larger firms.	Same as above with one to five years' experience in computer security.
EDP security consultant	Government, user companies, computer manufacturers, software houses, self-employment	Designs and integrates computer security systems and programs. Participates in formulating EDP security policy. Develops innovative solutions.	EDP security analysts; junior consultants with larger firms; teachers or researchers in computer security.	Same as above with record of proven accomplishment.

EDP = electronic data processing.

References

ASIS Foundation. *Career Opportunities in Security and Loss Prevention*. Washington, DC: ASIS Foundation.

Astor, Saul D. 1978. *Loss Prevention: Control and Concepts*. Boston: Butterworth Heinemann.

Buzby, Walter J. 1976. *Hotel and Motel Security Management*. Boston: Butterworth Heinemann.

Carroll, John M. 1987. *Computer Security*, 2nd ed. Boston: Butterworth-Heinemann.

Chuvala III, John and Robert James Fischer, eds. 1991. *Suggested Preparation for Careers in Security/Loss Prevention*. Dubuque, IA: Kendall/Hunt.

Colling, Russell L. 1982. *Hospital Security*, 2nd ed. Boston: Butterworth Heinemann.

Cunningham, William; John 1. Strauchs; and Clifford Van Meter. 1990. *The Hallcrest Report 11: Private Security Trends 1970-2000*. Boston: Butterworth-Heinemann.

Kaverman, Steven. 1990. "2000 and Beyond," *Security Management*. September.

Keller, Steven R. 1998. "Technology: Unlocking the Future for Security Practitioners," in *Suggested Preparation for Careers in Security/Loss Prevention*, John Chuvala III and Robert James Fischer, eds.

Langer, Steven. 1996. "The Wages of Security," *Security Management*. August.

Leader, Stefan H. 1997. "The Rise of Terrorism," *Security Management*. April.

Mack, Toni. 1984. "Looking Out for Number One," *Forbes*. 31 December.

Security. 1989. "Exploring Security Trends,*" Security*. February.

CHAPTER 2

CAREERS IN INVESTIGATIONS

J. Branch Walton
Lockmasters Security Management

This section explains how investigative positions exist in every area where security, loss prevention, safety, or risk management responsibilities occur. Investigations is imperative to finding causation and ultimate responsibility for crime, accidents, and all types of rule violations- Educational requirements are discussed- Both those that are necessary and specialty areas.

"Things may come to those who wait, but only the things left by those who hustle." Those aspiring to become investigators in the field of law enforcement or private security would do well to remember these words of Abraham Lincoln. These careers are becoming more professional, are receiving higher pay and thus are becoming more competitive each year. Everything one can do to make himself or herself stand above the other qualified applicants, is going to put them one step closer to getting hired by the employer of their choice.

This reading is an attempt to provide some guidance to those wishing to become investigators with government agencies or private industry. It will provide a general discussion on what agencies, departments, or companies are looking for in applicants and will offer some suggestions for making oneself a better qualified applicant.

Crimes of the Future

There appears to be no questions in any one's mind that the fastest growing areas of concern in the criminal justice - security fields are computer fraud, drug violations and terrorist acts. All three are critical concerns to our country.

It is estimated that the U.S. contains about 5% of the world's population and 60% of its drug problems. The U.S. is the most advanced nation in the production and use of computers and because of its wealth and position as a world leader, it is a major target of acts of terrorism. It stands to reason, therefore, that the law enforcement and security needs (career opportunities) will be for applicants with backgrounds or aptitudes related to these areas.

Law Enforcement - Security Careers of the Future

The number of investigator positions in law enforcement and private security is continually growing. Salaries are improving due to the caliber of personnel who are entering these fields. The positions are becoming more competitive, and the education required to obtain employment is going up throughout the country.

Most federal investigator positions require a college degree. Many state police agencies require a college degree, or 2 years of college, as do some city police departments or major university police departments. Your first obvious step in the area of formal education preparation is to determine the minimum education requirements of the organizations you are considering and obtain that education. It is important to keep in mind that obtaining the required education will not guarantee you employment. This will only bring you up to the level of all the other qualified applicants. For instance, this could mean you are now one of 300 applicants applying for 10 positions.

When actors or singers audition for a part, they seek something to make themselves stand out from the others auditioning for that position. You should use the same philosophy when applying for your career position. Obtain knowledge, skills, degrees, qualities, etc. beyond the job requirements that will benefit your prospective employer so that you will stand out from the other applicants. Career opportunities are there and are growing in number. Entry level standards for these positions are also increasing and more than ever, one must plan ahead if he or she hopes to be a viable applicant for the more desirable positions.

William Johnson of the Hudson Institute, on commenting about careers, stated that the jobs of tomorrow will belong to those "who can read, write and think."

The trend is for strong growth in private security areas. Private security operations can perform a tremendous public service, and there is no evidence that the public is not just as happy with private security personnel as with sworn law enforcement personnel in areas of similar patrolling. Private security can be an effective supplement to public police agencies.

Some police agencies are currently contracting out to private agencies for such services as towing, parking lot patrolling, traffic control and special event security. This growth is creating more career opportunities in the security/loss prevention areas.

There is a wide variety of investigation related positions available to those interested in this area. Many exist that are unknown to those already working in similar areas. Some exist in areas not traditionally thought of as investigator positions such as risk management, compliance, inspectors, quality control, safety, etc. Most large governmental agencies have a variety of investigator related positions, though some may be small in terms of total positions.

Insurance companies, hospitals, utility companies, credit card companies, department stores, major manufacturers, the transportation industry, etc., are all potential employers of those seeking careers in this area.

Perhaps your first serious investigative assignment could begin right now. Open the yellow pages of the phone book, locate numerous larger employers in your area, and attempt to identify all the investigative related positions they offer. An initial response from someone in the personnel department may be "none," as most will be thinking of the traditional security or criminal investigator positions. Such a response will necessitate further inquiries on your part.

14

Conduct more interviews. Determine your objectives. Remain flexible. Take good notes. Expect frustrations but keep inquiring. Evaluate your results. If you want to be an investigator of any sort, get used to this process.

Desired Background of Investigator Applicants

The success of an investigator depends on his ability to analyze, organize, use logic, operate independently, and especially on his/her ability to deal with people and properly record (report writing) investigative results. An investigator needs social skills -- to get along with people, talk, inquire, influence, and listen. These "social skills" can be acquired. The more you practice the better you get. Like good manners, it can be learned.

Fortunately for most municipal police departments, county and some state agencies, their investigators are obtained from their uniform ranks thus providing the employer the advantage of time to evaluate the skills of potential investigators. Most federal agencies hire their investigators from outside their departments, thus putting more pressure on the applicant to prove himself as a highly qualified applicant in a short period of time.

Law enforcement agencies and private security positions may vary on the entrance requirements, but generally they can be broken down to three areas.

1. Education: Requirements vary, but usually any major is acceptable where a college degree is needed. Some recommended courses are: computer science, foreign languages, accounting, English composition, law, sociology, psychology, debate/speech and forensic science.

2. Experience: Few entry level investigative positions in law enforcement or private security require any specific prior employment. Most, however, do desire a background in some field providing experiences dealing with a variety of people, such as teaching, sales or even waiter/waitress work. All positions such as these provide valuable lessons in evaluating, questioning, confronting and persuading people, the social skills mentioned earlier. The most desirable prior employment experience is, of course, in a similar type of investigative position but one must not overlook the opportunities for obtaining benefits from seemingly unrelated occupations. If these benefits do not appear to provide much edge in the selection process, their value will become evident once you become an investigator. Any employment experience related to the recommended college courses listed above is valuable.

3. Personal Demeanor/Character: The application process almost always includes an extensive interview or interviews. During these interviews, one should keep in mind the usual interview etiquette provided by so many guidelines. Don't underestimate the value of neatness, dress, manners, language and openness. Physical fitness and appearance are also important.

If you provide a resume or a company, agency, or department application form, make sure it is typed and complete. Sloppiness, misspelling and incompleteness on an application can terminate your chances immediately. A potential employer's first introduction to applicants is often through the applicant's resume or application, and more than likely, it is one of many applications. The only knowledge that company or agency has of you is through those papers. If you "look" sloppy and unable to follow instructions, your application process can end in less than a minute.

There is a constant need for minorities in the investigative units of law enforcement agencies and private security. This has nothing to do with EEO (Equal Opportunity Employment) guidelines or quotas. There is a definite shortage and need for qualified Afro-Americans, females, Orientals, Hispanics, etc. within most agencies / companies. Excellent career opportunities exist for those interested.

There is one solid piece of advice that needs to be given now. If you sincerely desire to have a career as an investigator, <u>STAY AWAY FROM DRUGS.</u> I know of few quicker ways to be refused employment in police work or private security than that of having been involved in the use (not to mention dealing) of illegal drugs. If this is the employment you seek, you need to make this "just say no" commitment early in your life.

Networking

Networking is a valuable employment seeking tool and should receive specific consideration by those seeking a career with law enforcement or private security. Get to know as many people as possible within the fields of interest to you. Develop a picture of their perfect applicant and use self motivation to strive to become that perfect applicant. When application time comes, through your time spent with your company or department acquaintances, you will know if it is truly the career you want, and they will know personally of your character and potential. This can be a major method of setting yourself above all the other applicants. You will also learn about other possible career opportunities while networking or associating with those already in investigative positions.

The grapevine is alive and active in these occupations when it comes to knowing who is hiring, pay, qualifications, and job descriptions. Networking can provide you with such information.

To learn of other potential opportunities, read classified sections of trade magazines and papers, request information brochures from agencies, departments or companies, and interview whenever possible. The Federal Law Enforcement Training Center (FLETC) at Glynco, Georgia, is the training site for the basic training of Federal law enforcement agencies, except the FBI and DEA. It is a good source for finding exactly which Federal departments employ investigators or uniform law enforcement personnel. Many departments may also employ "compliance" personnel. These are investigative related positions that check on the compliance of specific laws and regulations and refer any major violations to the law enforcement branch of their agencies. Agencies that have these compliance positions might also provide career development opportunities. The internet is now a major resource in job searches.

Finally, use networking conscientiously, by letting those in the investigative "circles" know you are looking. They can be excellent look outs and sources of referral. It should go without saying, however, that this should be handled with some caution with the security of your current employment in mind.

In the private security field, joining ASIS (American Society for Industrial Security) can provide networking opportunities. Student memberships are available. Several security magazines are available and provide excellent articles regarding careers with private industry.

Visiting universities with large law enforcement departments may provide insight into who is hiring. Most will, of course, give preference to their own students when offering assistance, but most will also willingly provide valuable guidance to all making inquiries. If majoring in law enforcement or security administration, inquire into intern programs. Keep in touch with classmates who begin employment in related positions. Use the internet.

Law

Successful prosecution is a direct result of quality investigations and quality investigations come from knowing the law. A formal education in the area of law enforcement, security administration, social justice or law is certainly a benefit when applying for a career as an investigator, but rarely is it a requirement. Most, if not all, prospective employers will train you in these areas after you are hired.

Knowledge of laws, the violations of which you will be investigating, is essential, but this can also be taught by your employer. The point is, as mentioned earlier, one should not disqualify himself/herself from a potential career as an investigator, merely because of an education centered around a seemingly unrelated area.

More Suggestions

Another suggestion for self development, and setting yourself above those other applicants, is to learn all you can about current fraudulent activities in general, and new investigative, forensic or scientific methods. Private security employers may be interested in your knowledge of new areas such as facsimile machine fraud, biometric access control devices or current hot topics such as computer fraud, business information theft, espionage, crisis management or workers compensation fraud. Law enforcement agencies could be interested in your knowledge of Automated Fingerprint Information System (AFIS), deoxyribonucleic acid (DNA) or hair analysis.

Three areas specifically come to mind when considering an applicant's background: accounting, computer training and foreign language capabilities. Outside of possessing the intangible aptitude or potential of being a good investigator, it is difficult to think of many qualities more desirable than these three. All can be of benefit to any investigative department at one time or another. There is a constant need for people (investigators) with these abilities.

The great influx of Hispanic, Asian and other foreigners to this country is not expected to end soon. The need for investigators with fluency of Spanish, Vietnamese, Japanese, Russian, etc. is obvious. There is a great sense of personal satisfaction present in those who speak more than one language.

In a recent study of a number of security decision makers, over half said they encountered some difficulty in hiring entry-level management personnel who met their requirements. One of the reasons for this difficulty was the lack of knowledge of computers and computerized equipment by the applicants.

One can gain experience, training or education through any number of sources: college, adult education courses, community education courses, military, other employment, hobbies, clubs, readings and a variety of other self education methods limited only by your imagination. The military services offer decent pay and excellent training, especially if you can get the occupational speciality of your choice.

Some federal agencies seek applicants only after they reach their mid or late twenties. The maturation process of the average person during their early 20's is very noticeable. A mature, college educated, 26-28 year old, with 5-7 years of experience in the work force is an attractive candidate to these agencies. If you are a young, recent graduate and intend to pursue employment with one of these agencies, this 5-7 year period can provide an excellent opportunity for you to better control your destiny through purposeful self directed education in the areas most in demand by your prospective employer. In my opinion, the single most beneficial area for those seeking federal employment (assuming all other requirements have been met) is a fluency in a second language.

As already stated, part of your self improvement plan should be to talk to as many people as you can in the agencies, departments, or industry, with whom you are interested. Get a description of their ideal applicant and use their descriptions as guidelines to improve your marketability. It should be mentioned that although a specific program of study may not be a requirement for employment that leads to an investigator position, those students specifically seeking entry level positions in private industry would certainly benefit by concentrating on security administration related courses.

There are some distinctions between the philosophy of law enforcement careers and careers in private security that should be mentioned. There are many exceptions, but generally the operational philosophy of law enforcement agencies is reactive, and private security is proactive. The ultimate motive of private industry is profit. The ultimate motive of law enforcement is arrest and prosecution. If a student is particularly interested in private security careers, some business knowledge would certainly be beneficial. If the student is concentrating on law enforcement as a career, perhaps a criminal justice administration course might be more helpful for those non-criminal justice majors.

Networking is especially important in private security, as the investigator in private industry does not have the same support available to the law enforcement investigator. When employed with a company, you must learn the corporate structure and where you fit in the structure. Interfacing is extremely important in developing your professional image and your image is ultimately determined by your own attitude toward your profession.

A recent survey conducted by JDG Associates, Ltd. Bethesda, MD, solicited opinions of American Society for Industrial Security (ASIS) leaders about trends in security hiring. The results could be valuable to those considering a career in the growing private security field. The figures below identify the percentage of those who used each method of recruiting sources to find new hires.

Employee referrals	79%
Advertising	75%
College recruiting	25%
Job fairs	20%
Internet	18%
Recruiting firms	15%
Resume services	8%
Open houses	6%

It is anticipated that the Internet will become a much greater recruiting resource in the near future so it makes sense to become familiar with its usage.

The above mentioned survey also rated the importance of various credentials deemed helpful to job attainment. They are ranked here in order of value according to those surveyed. Duplicate numbers indicate ties.

1. Security management experience
2. Masters or MBA
3. BA or BS
4. Certified Protection Professional (CPP) designation
5. Computer degree
6. General management experience
7. Certified Fraud Examiner (CFE) designation
7. Doctorate
7. AA degree
8. Engineering degree

Other credentials mentioned as helpful but less valuable than those above were law enforcement and military experience, other certifications and a security clearance.

Another category of interest from the JDG Associates, Ltd's <u>Year 2000 Security Management Job Opportunity Survey</u> covered fields where security opportunities were expected to be most available.

- Infotech, computer security
- Contract security and investigations
- Electronic and alarms
- Health care
- Education/teaching
- Lodging/resort
- Government services
- Retail/commercial
- Transportation/distribution
- Government
- Utility security
- Industrial

The above study results are available in the November 1998 issue of OMAA's Security Directors Report.

Another survey conducted by J. Branch Walton with members of the International Security Management Association (ISMA) in 1997 covered academic courses most recommended by members that would best prepare candidates for a successful security leaders position. The results emphasized the importance of a general business background in this occupation. Courses such as accounting and auditing, business organization, management, and writing skills were emphasized.

Summary

There are some excellent career opportunities as an investigator with local, state and federal law enforcement agencies as well as in private security. Pay and professionalism are improving, and competition for these positions is increasing. Many entry level positions require college degrees but few if any require any specific major.

If you desire a career in this field, identify the entry requirements and acquire them. Then seek additional qualities desirable to the prospective employer. Especially, seek some background in the area(s) of accounting, computers and a foreign language. Above all, stay away from illegal drugs. Develop your interview and other social skills. Improve your writing skills and be concerned about your physical fitness, and general appearance.

Constantly continue your learning process. This is your responsibility. Self directed learning refers to a self-motivated and self-managed planning process that you can use to learn, change and improve. This process should be not just pre-employment preparation, but should continue throughout your career. Ask, inquire and plan. You are the key to the success of your development.

CHAPTER 3

COMMUNICATION SKILLS -- PLAY A CRITICAL ROLE IN SECURITY LOSS MANAGEMENT

David R. Stratton, CPP

A person who is not able to communicate effectively will not only have problems achieving their goals on the job, but they will probably not be able to advance within management. It has been estimated that 75 to 80 percent of the information that is given from a supervisor to those in the line (or subordinates in general) is done verbally. The ability to speak well will enhance a persons chances to succeed.

The ability to write clear and effective reports and to give oral presentations are skills that should be mastered if you intend to have a successful career as a police officer or security professional. Obtaining a college degree does not necessarily mean students posses the oral and writing skills necessary to perform the job. In fact, it is common to find college graduates that can only read and write at the elementary level and couldn't begin to make an oral presentation even if they had thorough knowledge of the topic. Very often employers will examine the student's course curriculum and discover the student never completed any oral communication, writing courses, or additional English courses, beyond those that meet the general education requirements of the university.

I don't think students who are planning to enter the security field realize that they are cheating themselves in the long run by avoiding classes that will improve writing and speaking ability. Speaking from experience as one who originally sidestepped basic grammar and any other class that had an English prefix, I discovered, before it was too late, that the inability to communicate well, both orally and through writing, would most likely result in my not being promoted into a top management position. Poor verbal and written skills imply poor education and have a direct bearing on the level of position that you might be able to obtain from any employer. Upper management positions within a corporation or law enforcement agency demand individuals who can gain the respect of their superiors, peers, and subordinates. Part of that respect comes from their ability to write evaluations, letters, memos, and reports, lead discussions and meetings, and give presentations. Police detectives and security investigators must be able to properly document case files, write investigative notes, reports and statements, and testify at hearings, arbitrations, and trials concerning the results of their investigations. There are often situations when a judge, jury, or arbitrator must decide a case based on the word of the investigator against the word of the defendant. Poor writing skills, sloppy report writing, and the inability to communicate confidence and integrity through oral testimony, all breed doubt, which may allow a guilty subject to go free. Even the line employees such as the police officer or security guard must be able to write patrol reports, incident reports, and statements, and may also be required to testify in court or make oral presentations to supervisory personnel so that appropriate disciplinary action can be taken against an employee. Writing and speaking skills are critical to performing the job.

Good writing skills and oral communication skills are critical, not only as they apply to conducting investigations and giving testimony, but when dealing with employees, clients, and customers. Don't be fooled into thinking that law enforcement agencies that operate in the public sector don't have clients and customers the same as any private business. The people who reside, visit, or work in the businesses that make up a community are, in fact, the customers of police personnel who are sworn to protect and serve. Likewise, the customers of a security organization in the private sector are the employees and contractors that make up the business. The victims of crime become the clients of the police department or security organization. Good communications skills and writing ability are positive reinforcements to the customer that the individual representing the community or business is competent and professional. Police and security organizations have learned that the customer's perception of the professional image of the entire organization rests upon the customer's interaction with one or a few representatives of the organization. Although I don't believe that a community as a whole would have a negative view of their police department based on the inability of a few officers to write and speak well, I do believe that enough minor, negative reactions will tarnish a positive image of the entire organization in the eyes of some of their customers. Examine the rural police force compared to the large metropolitan force. It is common to stereotype the rural police department as being less educated, less modern, and less efficient in solving big, complex crimes. A police officer with poor writing and speaking skills that is part of the rural force will only add credence to the stereotype of the department personnel being less educated. If you fulfill the expectations of your customers, their overall perception of you and your organization will be what the customer expected it to be, which may not be what it is in reality.

As a Security Manager of a moderately large corporation and the coordinator of a college internship program, I have had the opportunity to examine and evaluate the writing skills of hundreds of students and job applicants. I check applications and resumes for spelling, grammar, and word usage and automatically eliminate any candidate that is unable to write at a college graduate level. Don't kid yourself that I am the only employment decision maker that does this. I have read college internship term papers where it was obvious the student did not know when to use an apostrophe, did not know the difference between "there", "their", and "they're", and who wrote more than twenty lines of text in one run-on sentence. These indicators of poor writing skills will surface during job interviews and evaluations. On one occasion I had to obtain a copy of a police report which documented an arrest of an individual who had stolen property from an employee of my company. The officer who completed the report indicated that the subject stole a car stereo which he spelled numerous times throughout the report as "stirio." This report was signed by the police chief to indicate that he reviewed it and was aware of the case. The report became evidence during the criminal trial and subsequently, it became a public record. Naturally, the defense attorney wanted to know what a "stirio" was because the officer testified that a "stereo" was stolen. One should also be aware that the transcript of most trials, this one being no exception, become a public record. No, the subject was not freed on the technicality, but imagine the damage this one incident caused to the reputation of the police officer, the police chief, and the police department in general. Would you feel confident in this officer's ability to investigate, complete a report, and testify about a murder investigation that occurred in your community? How would you feel if it was his word against the defendant? The fact that the police officer in my example had poor writing skills, coupled with the fact that the police chief failed to correct the mistake and initialed the report, makes me question the competency of the department. When a juror questions competency, you call it reasonable doubt.

Poor writing and oral communication skills are a reflection of the individual first, the educational institution second, and the organization that hired the individual third. You can bet that if too many job applicants from a particular educational institution exhibit a lack of the proper tools to meet employment standards, the employer will halt recruitment activity from the institution. I don't want to give you the impression that this would occur solely on the basis of poor writing or oral communication skills, but I do want to convey that many large corporations and criminal justice agencies weigh an individual's educational and practical experience before making an employment or promotional decision, and your communication skills may play a role in that decision. Would you sign a contract to purchase valuable merchandise if it had a lot of misspelled words, slang terms, and improperly used words? Would you invest a large sum of money if the investment counselor appeared to be reading a sales pitch from a card and did not express sincere confidence in the investment? Likewise, would a law enforcement agency hire an officer whose oral communication skills indicated that he would have trouble speaking in front of numerous strangers such as a grand jury? Would a large corporation hire a security specialist that would be responsible for submitting monthly written reports to the general manager reflecting the status of all security investigations, if the individual could not demonstrate proper sentence structure, grammar, and word usage during the application and interviewing process? Any person wishing to enter the criminal justice industry knows the answer to these questions, yet many fail to properly prepare themselves.

Education and practical experience are the keys to developing good writing and oral communication skills. One of the most valuable courses that I attended in college was a course titled "Business Speech," which was designed to teach how to make presentations and provide briefings to executives, supervisors, peers, and subordinates. This helped me in both my law enforcement and security careers. There is not much difference in making a presentation to a police chief, commanding general, or the president of a corporation. Knowing how and being prepared were the key elements to my success in making presentations to VIP personnel. What about those occasions where you don't have time to prepare? Giving impromptu speeches in my basic oral communication course helped me in those times when the president of my company called me into his office to provide an immediate update about a security investigation or project. English composition and technical writing courses help to sharpen basic writing skills that will allow you to write clear and concise reports. However, if you don't put much effort into the course -- it's easy to slide by and maintain minimum standards -- don't expect to get much in return. You can always follow in the footsteps of the college graduate that typed his own resume which was full of misspelled words, poor grammar, improper word usage, and whose entire educational experience had been devoted to meeting the minimum requirements.

He never completely comprehended why he was only able to obtain an entry level contract security guard position at very low wages.

As I said before, poor writing and oral communication skills are not the sole basis an employer uses to reject candidates for employment or promotion, but they are key factors in the process. I won't attempt to persuade you that you cannot succeed within the criminal justice industry if you have inadequate communication skills because it is not true. However, why risk paying the price of having to accept a lower paying job, with less responsibilities than you are capable of managing, because you did not obtain the communication tools through education and practical experience that you needed to demonstrate for the position? If you are one of those individuals that do not possess the requisite writing or speaking ability, concentrate some of your studies and efforts toward completing courses that I outlined above. I believe that if you pay some dues, sooner or later you will realize the reward.

CHAPTER 4

THE IMPORTANCE OF SOCIOLOGICAL KNOWLEDGE TO THE SECURITY PROFESSIONAL

Thomas Tomlinson, Ph.D., Professor
Law Enforcement and Justice Administration, Western Illinois University

Understanding basic theories of sociology can help in formulating policies that can deter, or otherwise reduce, potential theft and deviant activity. An example of this might be that with the proper training, counseling, and reward systems in place, it is possible to show subordinates how to "get ahead." Theft, because of different values, social pressures, or lack of socialization or opportunities is going to happen, but it can be reduced in total number of occurrences.

In the workplace theft can he reduced by giving personnel the chance to be a team member, to see potential for advancement, to share in profits, and some "say" in the operation, and a chance to reach other various goals.

Sociology is the scientific study of human social interaction. These interactions include organizational, group, and face-to-face aspects. Thus, sociologists study family life, organizational networks, the relation of management to labor, as well as the relation of supervisor to worker, and worker to worker. The areas of study are limitless.

While that definition sounds a bit "dry," sociology and sociological knowledge provide exciting insights into all human behavior. Many of these insights, as I will try to demonstrate, are very useful to the security professional. Whether working an employee theft problem in large organizations or trying to reduce shoplifting in a retail store, your knowledge of human behavior is essential to your task. Armed with that knowledge, you are more effective and efficient in performing what is required of you. Of course, knowledge of the latest security technology and techniques is important, but always remember that all of this technology is used in social situations where people are interacting and forming ideas and feelings based on that interaction.

Ask Sociologists why they chose this profession and they will tell you they did so because they wanted to understand people and society. They want to know why society works the way it does. And, this is indeed what they do. They try to find the social reasons things are as they are.

Anyone working in a profession involved with people needs to understand those people in the most thorough way possible. To the extent that this understanding is based on scientific fact rather than "common sense," the more astute one will be in his/her dealings with people. Factual knowledge and understanding will be accurate, and therefore will help the security professional do his/her job in a way that achieves the desired results. It helps to know why people steal as much as it does to know how they do it.

That is what sociology is all about. Sociologists want to answer three basic questions: What? How? Why ? Answers to these questions provide an explanation of some form of human behavior. That explanation provides the essential understanding of social phenomena such as crime. If we can explain employee theft, then we can find ways to control it. Let me explain more fully what I mean.

The first question of explanation that must be answered is: 'What exists and what is it like?" This question is essential. For example, we must know how much and what kind of employee theft is occurring before we can do anything about it. Most people assume ("common sense") that almost all employees steal from their company. However, Hollinger and Clark (1983), in a sociological study, found the figure to be closer to thirty percent. That is a large difference that is important; but this knowledge also leads us to ask what it is about those 30% that allow or push them to steal. When we begin to look at this aspect, we are asking the 'Why?" question.

Once we know what these people are like, we can then ask: 'Why do these factors produce the effects they do?" (Doby, 1968). We may also ask the "How" question: "How do factors work and combine to produce the outcome?" The answers to the "why" and "how" questions are the explanation. The explanation allows us to search for causes in this instance employee theft. Knowing causes can be very useful for the security professional.

If we can find a cause for any crime, the strategy would be to eliminate the cause, thus eliminating the crime and the victim. This is not a popular view today, as it is often seen as "coddling criminals." However, the technique is well used in the medical sciences. In the fight against cancer or AIDS, the researchers are looking for causes (explanation) with the hope of finding a vaccine that will block the cause in the first place, thus preventing the disease. We can use the same logic in preventing crime (i.e. employee theft or shoplifting). Primary prevention before the crime occurs would be most desirable in that there would be no victim. Secondary prevention is a corrective/reactive strategy. A crime, and therefore a victim, must have occurred for the criminal justice or security system to step in. If the perpetrator is convicted he may be subjected to correctional or treatment strategies that usually do not work because they are based either on poor research, poor theory, or classical ideology. Primary prevention is the realm of security. Thus, knowledge of causes can have a direct effect on prevention of such crimes as employee theft or shoplifting.

You may ask what types of things can be causes of crime. Four broad types of causes have been identified (Boskff, 1972, Sheley, 1983). These include (1) motivation, (2) freedom from social restraints, (3) skill, and (4) opportunity. Let's briefly look at each of these in turn.

"Motivation" concerns the person's intention to commit a crime. If he wants to commit a crime, and the other factors are present, he will. "Freedom from social restraints" refers to the fact that all of us are kept from committing crime by fear of others (an external constraint) and because we have learned from childhood, it is wrong to steal (internal constraint). An organization can provide external constraints both formally (company rules) and informally (interaction with employees). A security professional knowledgeable about sociological ideas of cause would know however, that these constraints would not be enough to reduce theft. There may be no internal constraints on the employee or his motivation to commit crime may be overpowering. Other measures would have to be taken to ensure security.

"Skill" concerns the ability to commit a crime. Can the person put thoughts and acts together in a way that allows him to commit the crime? For example, an embezzler needs knowledge of accounting in order to commit the crime. Or, a shoplifter needs skills in hiding stolen objects, remaining calm and projecting a false image of himself to everyone else. A highly motivated criminal without skill will usually be caught. A good security professional should know the skills of the employees of the firm for which he/she works.

"Opportunity" is provided by anything in the environment that is conducive to the commission of a crime. For example, an opportunity for theft might be an unlocked storeroom. However, only the motivated person who felt little constraint would steal from it. Hollinger and Clark (1983) found that employees who felt constrained by the informal work group usually would not take advantage of the opportunity to steal when present. Therefore, you can see that opportunity is not enough for the security professional to be concerned with. He/she needs to understand all of the other factors we discussed as well.

I should also note here that the removal of opportunity when possible, has been found to be a much better crime reduction technique than so-called "deterrence" where the primary factor is fear. If a person is afraid, it is said, he will not commit a crime. However, sociological research has not found this to be so (Walker, 1998). Put differently, primary prevention in security must not only focus on opportunity (the realm of much security technology), but also on motivation, social constraint, and the skill of the offender. When all of these aspects are taken into account, a much more professional and effective security operation can take place.

Sociological knowledge provides us with many specific explanations that allow us to assess opportunity, motivation, skill, and social constraint. My goal here is to select several of the more important and recent sociological explanations, briefly describe each, and show its implications for security policy, practice, and prevention.

Merton's (1968) explanation of anomie is among the best known of the strain theories. Others include Cohen's (1955) and Cloward and Ohlin's (1960). All are different, yet all revolve around the ideal of strain. Basically, Merton argued that anomie (normlessness, or lack of rules) exists in the U.S. because legitimate goals are held out to everyone as being attainable, while all the legitimate means for reaching those goals are unequally distributed. The American Dream of success is desirable to all; but for those who have no means to reach it, or whom feel their opportunities are blocked, adaptations to anomie are a possibility. The adaptation of concern here is "innovation" where the person keeps the goals but rejects the legitimate means for use of illegitimate means (usually criminal). Thus, a poor worker under the strain of low wages might steal from the company, as would the business executive who felt he was not living up to success goals, which the company did not provide (Merton, 1968). In addition, a lower class person under strain might be a prime candidate to shoplift.

Cohen's (1955) explanation locates the source of strain as beginning in loss of esteem of working class boys as they were compared to middle class peers. Cloward and Ohlin's theory price the source of strain on a sense of injustice brought about by blocked legitimate and illegitimate opportunities (1960).

A new and useful theory by Messner and Rosenfeld (1997, 1995) extends Merton's Anomie theory by looking at the fact that the economy dominates life in the U.S. and interferes with the functioning of other social institutions. They, like Merton, begin their analysis by looking at the "American Dream" which they define as "Commitment to the goal of material success, to be pursued by everyone in society, under conditions of open, individual competition" (1997:62). With Merton, they argue that anomie stems from the same basic values upon which the American Dream rests. These values include achievement, individualism, universalism and excessive emphasis on monetary rewards.

Achievement refers to the fact in American culture, people are evaluated by what they have achieved; monetary success being the basic measure of what society thinks one is worth. This promotes the mentality that "it is not how you play the game, but whether you win or lose" (1997:63). Individualism refers to the idea that in the U.S. people must "make it on their own." In this atmosphere, people are considered competitors in the struggle to achieve rewards. This pressure makes people disregard the rules when the rules interfere with the attainment of personal success goals. Universalism occurs when everyone is supposed to aspire to the same success goals and are entitled to "dream" about success. This also means, however, that failure is unacceptable for anyone. Thus, there is great pressure to "win: at all costs", and anomie can exist within the entire social structure not just the lower class. The "fetishism" of money refers to the fact that success in American culture is shown by the accumulation of monetary rewards more than any other attribute. Money and its accumulation are considered the measure of success and it has no bounds because it is always possible to have more money. Messner and Rosenfeld argue that these cultural characteristics provide for anomie in society, and therefore high levels of crime (1997:64).

These authors further define how this anomie situation works. They point out that the U.S. has several necessary social institutions that are supposed to function somewhat separately from each other in providing a stable social life. These institutions are the family, education, and the polity. However, in a society that overemphasizes the goal of money, anomie results from what is called the "institutional balance of power." Given the factors described above, all goals other than monetary success are secondary and thus the "institutional balance of power" is tilted toward the economy (1997:7), while private gain becomes the organizing principle for all social life.

This economic dominance is shown in three different ways. First is "devaluation" where non-economic goals and positions are devalued in the family, polity, and education. For example, schools are not a place to learn knowledge, but to prepare for a job. "Accommodation" refers to the fact that other institutions become structured to accommodate economic roles. For example, the family cannot exist without paid employment. "Penetration" of economic norms into other institutional areas is the third factor. For example, in schools, learning takes place within the context of competition for rewards.

Thus, when American society is oriented toward an unrestrained pursuit of economic success to an extreme degree, with other institutions having secondary importance, anomie is the result. An environment is created in which the social rules are not able to regulate people and external social controls cannot be provided by other institutions. The result of this is a high rate of crime. Legitimate means to reach the elusive success goals are never felt to be adequate, so illegal activity will often be attractive, and the structural supports from other institutions will be inadequate to control it. Weak institutions also invite crime as more people question their authority in an anomic society.

Messner and Rosenfeld have shown why there are high levels of crime in American society, but they also offer some suggestions for crime reduction. If we have high levels of anomie and weak social controls, then crime control "requires transformation from within, a reorganization of social institutions, and a regeneration of cultural commitments" (1997:96).

Families need to be revitalized, as well as the schools and the polity. Their goals should be enhanced so they can assume more social control. For example, family leave, job sharing, flexible work schedules, and employer provided child care would help relieve the anomic situation by helping the family reassert its influence. In addition, other cultural goals can be emphasized. For example, schools can be given enough money to do their job properly. From the standpoint of reducing employee theft, the employer can implement some of the above ideas in the workplace, thus reducing the effects of anomie on the individual worker and as a result, their motivation to steal. This again is primary prevention.

Robert Agnew developed yet another anomie theory that is really a "strain" theory. According to this theory, when goals are blocked, a person feels strain or frustration, which increases his/her likelihood of committing crime. Agnew broadened his theory to include more sources of strain beyond blocked goals. His first source of strain is "the failure to achieve positively valued goals". Included here are three subtypes. The first is similar to other anomie theories. Here strain is a disjunction between aspirations and actual achievement or expectations. The second type sees strain as disjunction between expectations and actual achievement. Here the focus is on what people expect based on past experience, and what they actually achieve. If expectations are not met, strain is produced. Third, strain can be a disjunction between just/fair outcomes and actual outcomes. Here, as long as an outcome of a person's efforts are considered fair and equitable, strain will not be produced.

A second major source of strain is "removal of positively valued stimuli from the individual." Loss of a job, or anticipation of loss, is one such strain producer. Others could include loss of benefits or demotion to a lower job.

A third major source of strain is the "presentation of negative stimuli." A person will feel strain when something negative happens and will seek to avoid it, end it, or seek revenge. Negative relations at home are obvious when abuse is concerned. However, negative relations in the workplace can also cause strain. This type of strain requires no specific goals on the part of the person.

Agnew argues that each type of strain could create a predisposition for crime, which could be acted upon in certain situations. These situations are usually ones where the strain has been chronic and long lasting. In such a case, even a slight negative situation may produce criminal behavior. Agnew discusses several adaptations a person can make to strain, but the point here is clear. To reduce employee theft, the workplace must avoid the types of strain Agnew describes. This is the primary prevention. In addition, situations that would allow for easy crime commission should be avoided. That is, security practices should be instituted to reduce the possibility of theft. This is primary prevention that attempts to reduce motivation to commit crime.

Hollinger and Clark (1983) illustrate how these principles work concerning employee theft. They found that younger workers were much more likely to commit theft than were older workers. From their interviews with these workers, the researchers found that younger workers felt more strain because of lower pay and little seniority. In other words, they felt anomie -- a feeling that the rules did not apply under these circumstances. Hollinger and Clark's recommendation for theft reduction was to integrate the young offenders into the workplace more fully. This may include giving them more pay; but integration would also alleviate any feelings of injustice that might be there. In fact, Hollinger and Clark argue that a lack of consensus on standards of behavior in the workplace can often exist. Workers can be anomie – not knowing what is expected of them. Combined with any sort of strain, employee theft will occur. Primary prevention would include reduction of strain and opportunities to be criminal. Note that anomie/strain theories are concerned with motivation (strain), and a lack of social constraints (anomie) as the critical elements of criminal explanation. As we will see, others approach these factors differently.

Differential association is a form of learning theory (Sutherland and Cressey, 1978). It argues that crime is learned in intimate personal groups. This includes the learning of techniques (skills), motives, rationalizations, and drives.

The theory claims that a person will commit crime when he/she has an excess of these definitions over non-criminal definitions. In a complex society, a person will receive both kinds of definitions, but he/she will become criminal only if there is an excess of those favorable to crime. On a primary preventive policy level, children especially should be kept away from criminal definitions. These are all around them -- in televisions, books, and parents. It is the parent's primary duty to provide more and higher intensity non-criminal definitions.

In the workplace, not only should employees with criminal definitions be identified by the security officer; but also it ought to be made clear by management and co-workers that crime of any form will not be tolerated. This may not be easy. Management cannot expect its rules to be obeyed unless the supervisors and workers agree that it is the proper thing to do. The definitions learned in face-to-face interaction are the strongest in the workplace (see Hollinger and Clark, 1983). The definition of the situation will determine the attitudes toward thefts and other crimes. A collective anti-crime consensus in the work situation is the best way to reduce theft.

Note that differential association deals with motivation (learning of motives, rationales), internal constraints (whether learned or not), external constraints (the agreed upon definitions), skills (in terms of the situations in which they are learned). Opportunity is not dealt with in this theory.

Hirschi's social control theory (1969) has a broad base of empirical support. It, as the others, does not try to differentiate between different types of criminals, but does concern itself with different degrees of involvement in criminal activity. Basically, Hirschi argues that if we are effectively socialized, we will form the social bonds of attachment, commitment, involvement, and belief. Each of these bonds in turn lead to a stake in conformity, which would prohibit criminal behavior. To the extent the bonds are broken, the person would be free to deviate and commit crime.

The nature of each bond is important (Hirschi, 1969). Attachment is defined as the ties of liking and loving that the person has with others. The family is the main source of these ties, but peers and schools also play a major role. Commitment is the time, energy and self invested in conventional activities. Involvement refers to engrossment in conventional activities that lead toward conventional success. The more committed a person is, the less likely he is to commit crime. Belief refers to the person's acceptance of the societal valued system and laws. Obviously, if a person accepts the laws as valid, he will be less likely to become criminal.

While social control theory argues that the four bonds are developed in family groups, they are also nurtured in other social situations such as the workplace. To the extent that attachment, commitment, involvement, and belief can be nurtured, the security professional will find less theft and other crimes occurring. Obviously, a person who feels attached to his job will be less likely to commit crimes against the company. Hollinger and Clark (1983) point out that when employees feel that they are not trusted, they are more likely to be deviant, while employees who feel that they are trusted are less likely to be so.

A mutual feeling of trust is really part of the attachment bond. Commitment can be produced by keeping employees informed of, and involved with, long-range company goals. Profit sharing and employee assisted management are two mechanisms that could accomplish this. To the extent the security professional can foster this bond, he/she will have decreased potential criminality. Involvement, in terms of keeping employees occupied with relevant and interesting work, would also tend to reduce deviance. The employee has too great a stake in conforming to risk it for the sake of stealing a few objects. Belief cannot be constructed in the workplace; but it can be reinforced. Formal rules are necessary. However, to be effective, the employees need to be gently reminded of them often (Hollinger and Clark, 1983). This can serve to reinforce the basic belief structure of the individual.

Social control theory fits in well with the critical elements of explanation. This is the only explanation that deals directly with "freedom from social constraints." As noted, the theory argues that, without social bonds, people feel free to deviate. The bonds, therefore, are the constraints. Attachment, commitment, and involvement are combined internal/external constraints, while belief is synonymous with internal constraints. Motivation is addressed in social control theory as well. The person will be motivated to conform due to the strengths of the attachment bond. Skill and opportunity are not really addressed by this theory.

Here again we see that the security professional needs to know much more than technological knowledge. Knowledge of people's social bonds, in this case, can help ensure the major goals of primary prevention.

Hirschi's original (1969) theory emphasized that social bonds were created by "indirect" control by parents. However, Gottfredson and Hirschi (1990) emphasize "direct" control by parents. Unless parents punish misbehavior and closely monitor their children, the child will not develop self-control and will have a greater propensity to criminality and analogous acts. In other words, a person will commit crime if he/she has low self-control and criminogenic situations are present.

Defining crime as "acts of force or fraud undertaken in pursuit of self-interest," Gottfredson and Hirschi argue that crime provides immediate gratification of desires (1990:15). People with low self-control respond to the immediate environment and do not defer gratification. Criminal acts fulfill these immediate desires. Since people with low self-control lack diligence, crime for them provides easy, simple gratification. Low self-control people do not have long term occupational pursuits, and usually are low in skills. Crime for them requires little skill or planning. People with low self-control are unkind and do not care about others. Hence, their crime may be likely to produce pain or discomfort.

This pattern is quite different from other theories. The authors acknowledge that, but argue that most crime fits this mold. It is unspecialized, low-level law breaking that is done mostly for relief of momentary irritation (1990:90).

As the authors note: "In sum, people who lack self-control will tend to be impulsive, insensitive, physical (as opposed to mental), risk-taking, short sighted, and nonverbal, and they will intend therefore to engage in criminal and analogous acts" (1990:90).

Individuals with low self-control do not learn it later in life. That is why the stress is placed on the family. By the time one is ready for employment, it is too late to develop self-control. People with low self-control may commit many non-criminal acts that are "on the edge" such as sky diving, drag racing, gambling, etc. The authors see these as equivalents to crime in terms of behavior. When people do not consider the consequences of their actions and crime becomes more likely.

Self-control theory argues therefore, that offenders can commit all types of crimes and do not specialize. White-collar criminals are no different from others. Most white-collar crimes, like employee theft, provide a quick and certain benefit with little effort. They do require opportunity. A person with low self-control, when given the opportunity to steal will steal. However, the authors argue that the requirements to hold most jobs are related to high self-control. If this is the case, there should be little employee theft. Indeed, Hollinger and Clark (1983) found that most people did not commit employee theft. They also found that the highest rate of employee thefts was reported by younger employees. These are the employees most likely to exhibit low self-control and to be fired early.

To reduce employee theft according to this theory, one needs to reduce opportunity for theft, and hire employees or managers who have been socialized to accepted values inside and outside business that forbid stealing. This theory deals with social constraints and opportunity, as well as motivation.

Labeling theory is another form of social explanation of crime that can be useful to security professionals (Lemert, 1951, 1972). The theory is concerned with the effect of people's reactions to a criminal act and the subsequent development of a criminal career (Lemert, 1972). A person may commit a primary deviance and be caught. He may then become labeled as bad and have his evil dramatized by others in society. After repeated episodes of this labeling and differential treatment, the person may come to view himself as deviant (see differential association above). The person may then engage in secondary deviance because he has reorganized his entire social self around a deviant role. He believes he is socially acceptable as a deviant and may continue to develop a long criminal career if the feedback process of negative societal reaction continues. That is, if a person is labeled as a deviant or criminal in a continuous manner, whether or not he actually is, he will begin to believe he is deviant and act accordingly.

This approach leads to several ideas concerning prevention. According to this point of view, the Security professional would be wise not to set up an atmosphere of accusation. He/she also should not accuse any individual of theft or other crimes without a great deal of factual evidence. A falsely accused person may decide that, since he/she is viewed as a criminal anyway, he. /she might as well commit criminal acts. This same logic could be applied to the entire workplace. Another example concerns shoplifting. If a person is falsely accused, the label may still stick to the point that the person is always viewed with suspicion by security personnel. Common knowledge would indicate that this practice should deter the person. However, it is just as likely that the person would accept the label, or say "what the hell" and engage in the criminal activity anyway. Sociological knowledge does not always follow common sense.

Labeling theory also alerts us to another situation. According to this point of view, people are constantly defining the situations they are in based on what they believe other people are thinking of them. The "other" people, in turn, are coming up with their definitions in exactly the same way. Both people then arrive at a mutually agreed upon "definition of the situation."

It has been found (Hollinger and Clark, 1983) that when there is no consensus in the workplace concerning what acceptable behavior is, employee theft increases. The tolerable amount of deviance in the workplace is negotiated between the supervisors and the workers.

Security personnel must know this and figure out ways to change the agreed-upon definitions. This cannot be done by strict imposition of the rules from the top down (Hollinger and Clark, 1983). Rather, to be effective, a new negotiated definition must be brought about. When this new definition is accepted the employee theft problem can be reduced dramatically according to the authors.

Labeling explanations address several critical elements of criminal explanation. Motivation is addressed by the person's acceptance of, and decision to live with, the label. It is also dealt with in terms of the negative labeling environment creating an excuse to commit crime. Also, a person so labeled may feel free of inner constraints and commit crime. A successful security professional should always be aware that his/her actions may have negative or unintended impact through labeling that can be counterproductive in reducing employee crime.

Routine activity theory has a different focus than any so far mentioned. It focuses on the opportunity for crime and thus compliments the other theories. Cohen and Felson (1979; see also Felson, 1998) argue that for crime to occur, there must be (1) a motivated offender, (2) suitable targets, and (3) the absence of capable guardians against violation. If these all occur at the same time, as people go about their "routine activities", crime is likely to occur. Routine activities could be job or family activities. For example, the job separates people from those they trust most (family) and puts them in more contact with different people and circumstances. The authors note especially that retail theft is most likely where goods are in retail establishments with heavy volume and few employees to guard it, satisfying conditions (1) and (2) above.

Routine activities theory is closely related to the crime prevention strategy "crime prevention through environmental design" (CPTED). According to this approach, suitable targets are to be minimized and guardians are to be properly placed. This involves looking at people's daily activities and relating those to crime opportunities.

The basic principles of CPTED are to control natural areas, provide natural surveillance, and foster territorial behavior (Felson, 1998:150). For example, placement of doors in appropriate areas may reduce theft. These CPTED design approaches apply three strategies. Natural strategies include design and layout of space to improve security. Organized strategies include security guards and police. Mechanical strategies include alarms, cameras and additional employees. Also included in CPTED is a temporal dimension. That is schedules, work hours, etc. are part of the environment to be designed. Some physical aspects of crime prevention would include target hardening (bolting down the computer), construction (use physical barriers to reduce unauthorized entry), and noise (alarms to scare off intruders).

The application of this theory is apparent in preventing employee theft. However, this is not primary prevention. This theory says little about the motivated offender. It only deals with opportunity. We can only install so many alarms, locks, and guards. The main point of crime reduction from the sociological perspective is again primary prevention.

The above paragraphs describe only several of the most prominent theory groups which sociologists use in explaining crime. There are many others, but these have been enough to illustrate my major points. Sociological knowledge is, and can be, very useful to security professionals. Sociological knowledge can be used to inform crime prevention techniques aimed at deterring the person from the criminal act after he/she decides to do it. Technological devices -- their usage and placement -- can be better used with knowledge of sociological principles.

However, my main point has been that this knowledge is also very useful to the security professional in terms of primary prevention -- keeping people from wanting to commit the crime in the first place. I have shown that by knowing what?, why?, and how?, we can obtain an explanation. This explanation defines the causes of the criminal activity. Primary prevention concerns eliminating these causes. Also, the causes fall into four different categories: motivation, freedom from social constraints, skill, and opportunity. I then showed how the dominant theories of the day address these issues in terms of employee theft and, in some cases, shoplifting.

Security professionals, armed with knowledge such as this, are in a much better position to do well in their jobs. Courses in sociology and other behavioral sciences can have a direct payoff for security personnel by helping them be more effective and efficient in their duties.

References

Agnew, Robert. 1992. "Foundation for a General Strain Theory of Crime and Delinquency." *Criminology.* Vol. 30.

Boskoff, Alvin. 1972. *The Mosaic of Sociological Theory.* New York: Crowell.

Cloward, Richard A., and Lloyd E. Ohlin. 1960. *Theory and Opportunity: A Theory of Delinquent Gangs.* New York: Free Press.

Cohen, Albert K. 1955. *Delinquent Boys.* New York: Free Press.

Cohen, Lawrence and Marcus Felson. 1979. "Social Change and Crime Rate Trends: A Routine Activity Approach." *American Sociological Review.* 44:588-608.

Doby, John T. 1969. "Logic and Levels of Scientific Explanation." Pp. 137 in *Sociological Methodology* edited by Edgar F. Borgatta.

Felson, Marcus. 1998. *Crime and Everyday Life.* Thousand Oaks, California:Pine Forge Press.

Gottfredson, Michael and Travis Hirschi. 1990. *A General Theory of Crime.* Stanford: Stanford University Press.

Hirschi, Travis. 1969. *Causes of Delinquency. Berkeley.* University of California Press.

Hollinger, Richard C. and John P. Clark. 1983. *Theft by Employees.* Lexington: D.C. Heath.

Lemert, Edwin M. 1951. *Social Pathology.* New York: McGraw-Hill.

Lemert, Edwin M. 1972. *Human Deviance, Social Problems and Social Control.* Englewood Cliffs, Prentice-Hall.

Merton, Robert K. 1968. *Social Theory and Social Structure.* New York: Free Press.

Messner, Steven and Richard Rosenfeld. 1997. *Crime and the American Dream.* Bellmont, California: Wadsworth.

Messner, Steven and Richard Rosenfeld. 1995. "Crime and the American Dream." *The Legacy of Anomie Theory.* vol. 6.

Sheley, Joseph F. 1983. "Critical Elements in Criminal Behavior Explanation." *Sociological Quarterly*, 24:509-525.

Sutherland, Edwin, and Donald R. Cressey. 1978. *Principles of Criminology.*, Chicago: Lippincott.

Walker, Samuel. 1998. *Sense and Nonsense about Crime: A Policy Guide.* Monterey, Calif.: Brooks/Cole.

CHAPTER 5

LEGAL ISSUES IN THE SECURITY/LOSS PREVENTION FIELD

Julie Gilmere, J.D.

The protection of people, property, and information requires careful planning, decision making, and action, all based upon and integral to the law.

Discussion of legal differences between public and private police, arrest powers, elements of crimes, rules of evidence, and criminal and civil liabilities are but a few of the topics which must be covered by any training program or courses for prospective security personnel.

A major difficulty in discussing the authority of private security officers is the diversity of the profession. The term "security officer" is one that encompasses a variety of individuals performing somewhat related duties in numerous situations. For example, there are at least three broad categories of personnel performing security duties: the private citizen, the commissioned citizen and the law enforcement officer performing in an off-duty capacity.

The authority of a security officer is based on tort, criminal, contract, constitutional, statutory and administrative law. Each will be briefly discussed.

Tort Law

The single most important regulation of authority of security personnel is tort law. A tort is a civil wrong, other than a breach of contract, for which money damages or an injunction may be given as a remedy. The common thread woven into all torts is the idea of unreasonable interference with the interests of others. The plaintiff is the injured individual(s) that brings a case to court, asserting the defendant is responsible for his injury. The person responsible for the plaintiff's injury is held liable because he acted with an unreasonable intention or because he departed from a reasonable standard of care. Tort law sets the legal standards that gauge the actions of security personnel. Tort law sets the parameters of permissible conduct by defining what activity is considered reasonable.

Criminal Law

Criminal law concerns wrong against society. While a tort is considered a private wrong and the remedy is a civil lawsuit brought by the injured party on his own behalf, a crime is a wrong against the public. The public, through its representative, the prosecutor, initiates action to punish the violator. Victims that were only a witness in criminal cases may now collect for actual losses; such as in assault and battery cases they can college expenses. Like the tort law, criminal law serves as a deterrent to improper action and thus sets limits on the actions of security personnel. The same act by a security officer can be both a tort and a crime. For, example, a security officer could be sued in civil court for an assault and battery as well as prosecuted for the same act in criminal court. A security officer's employer can be brought into the case to absorb the cost of damages if an employee's tort was committed within the scope of his employment. Victims that were only witnesses in criminal court can now collect for actual losses, such as in assault and battery cases. Losses can include medical costs, dental expenses and lost wages.

Contract Law

A contract is an agreement between two or more persons in which they exchange something of value, called "consideration." The agreement may be oral or written. One party promises to do, or to refrain from doing something, in exchange for a similar promise by the other party. If a party fails to abide by the agreement, the other party may sue in court and the judge can order the defendant to perform as required by the terms of the contract or may award money damages to the innocent party for the other party's breach of the contract. The parties to a contract can limit the authority of security personnel by providing that certain security procedures can not be used. For example, a contract might provide that security officers can not be in uniform or carry a nightstick, even though local law would permit it. On the other hand, contract language may grant authority to officers that they might not otherwise possess. For example, a labor contract might authorize the random search of employees as they leave the workplace. A contract cannot change responsibility for criminal violations or constitutional restrictions. Constitutional restrictions will be discussed next.

Constitutional Law

In general, provisions of the federal and of state constitutions do not apply to actions of private security officers because they are not government officials. Constitutional restrictions are designed to safeguard the rights of the public against abuse by governmental officials. For example, the Fourth Amendment of the United States Constitution prohibits unreasonable searches by police officers. The major remedy for such a violation is that courts will not permit the use of such evidence during a criminal trial. A private security officer who conducts an unreasonable search could be sued in civil court under a tort theory of invasion of privacy. The evidence would still be admitted in criminal court because private security officers are not subject to the constitutional limits that govern a government official. The problem with searches will be discussed later.

Statutory Law

Most states have enacted statutes which address the authority of security personnel in some way. Security personnel have the same power/authority as any other citizen, unless a state statute expands the authority. Expansion of their authority opens them up to increased liability for constitutional violations if their authority becomes closer to police authority. Some statutes establish standards for the qualifications and training of security personnel. Other statutes may indicate when citizens may arrest other citizens or when searches may be conducted. There are also statutes which allow merchants to detain shoplifters and statutes which regulate electronic eavesdropping. A violation of such laws may result in, an illegal arrest, the loss of the use of such evidence, and/or civil and criminal liability.

Administrative Law

Administrative law is the area of civil law that deals with the creation and activities of federal and state independent agencies and executive departments. These agencies are created by the legislature to regulate specific areas that need requirements and enforcement by the public sector. Many states have an agency which administers and enforces the licensing and regulation of persons engaged in security work. Rules made by agencies such as the National Labor Relations Board and the Occupational Safety and Health Administration impact on the conduct of the security officer in numerous private and public work settings.

If we examine the various sources of authority discussed above, we can make some generalizations with regard to a security officer's power to arrest, search, question suspects and use force. As previously noted, there will be differences in power because of the different categories of personnel providing security services in the United States. The discussion which follows emphasizes the powers of the "typical" security officer- a private citizen performing security duties for a private corporation.

Arrest Powers

Unless one is deputized, commissioned or is employed in a situation where a particular state statute applies, a security officer has no greater arrest power than that of the average citizen. Arrest powers do vary, however, depending on such factors as whether the crime committed was a felony or misdemeanor and whether the offense was committed within the arrester's presence.

In general, a citizen may arrest another for a felony which was in fact committed, even if not in the arrester's presence, where the arrester has reasonable grounds for believing the felony was committed. In those states which permit private citizens to arrest for misdemeanors, the offense usually must have been committed in the arrester's presence. Presence means that the arrester detected the violation through one of his senses at the time of occurrence.

The following are examples of statutes authorizing arrests by private persons:

A private person may arrest another: (1) for a public offense committed or attempted in his presence; (2) when the person arrested has committed a felony although not in his presence; (3) when a felony has been in fact committed, and he has reasonable cause for believing the person arrested to have committed it. California Federal Laws Annotated PC 837

Any person may arrest another when he has reasonable grounds to believe that an offense other than an ordinance violation is being committed. Illinois Compiled Statutes, 725 ILCS 5/107-3

A private person may make an arrest when a felony has been committed, in fact, and he has reasonable grounds to believe that the person being arrested has committed it. Kentucky Revised Statutes, section 431.005

[A]ny person may arrest another person (a) for a felony when the latter has in fact committed such felony, and (b) for any offense when the latter has in fact committed such offense in his presence. Consolidated Laws of New York CPL section 140.30

Possessing reasonable grounds to arrest is generally not a defense to a false arrest where the person taken into custody is not convicted of the offense for which arrested. The arrester is civilly liable if a crime was not actually committed. The reasonableness of the arrester's action is not a defense. In contrast, most police officers may arrest on the basis of reasonable grounds and the arrest is valid even though the suspect is not found guilty of the crime. Thus, the private officer has greater exposure to civil liability because of the public officer's broader arrest powers.

Search Powers

There are few cases which examine the legal right of private citizens to conduct searches. Where searches by security officers have been approved by the courts, they usually have been upheld on the basis of one of the following theories: consent search, search incident to a valid arrest or as part of a merchant's detention.

Where a consent search is possible, it is important to clearly define the scope of the permissible search. Where can the officer look? Such consent must be freely given and may be revoked at any time during the search.

Although a person may orally waive his legal protections concerning searches, it is recommended that whenever possible the consent be obtained in writing. The written permission is usually more persuasive evidence that the individual authorized the search.

Consent to search may be given by anyone legally in possession of the property. A major problem area in this regard are the third-party consent situations where someone other than the suspect gives permission to search. The key concept is whether the search intruded upon the suspect's reasonable expectation of privacy. For example, a search might be conducted of a locker used by a suspect at his place of employment. Who can authorize such a search? The employer will argue that it has the right to search because the locker is the property of the employer. The employee will argue that the locker is his because the employer has allowed him to use his own lock on it. If the employer has created an area of the workplace where the employee legitimately expects freedom from his employer's intrusion, then a search may constitute an invasion of privacy.

Searches in the work setting are frequently authorized by a pre-employment agreement which states that the applicant agrees to comply with all company rules and procedures. They may also be authorized by virtue of a collective bargaining agreement between the labor union and the management of the company. Because such agreements allow searches on the basis of a consent theory, and because consent may be revoked at any time, such agreements should not be relied upon to justify a search where an employee refuses to permit the search. Such cases should be handled administratively and the employee disciplined according to company policy, rather than force a non-consensual search.

As a practical matter, most searches are conducted on the basis of consent. Not too many people will resist a security officer's reasonable request to inspect a package or to look into a purse. In instances where consent is refused and the officer is sure that the person has committed a crime, it may be possible to arrest the individual and search him as part of the arrest.

It is a well-recognized exception to the Fourth Amendment search warrant requirement that public police officers may search an arrestee at the time of arrest. A number of courts have applied the same approach to arrests by private security officers. Courts that have permitted such searches frequently do so on the theory that the officer has the right to protect himself from arrestees who may be carrying weapons. In states where it is not clear whether such searches are permitted, the security officer should call for public law enforcement officer assistance. The responding police officers can then search the individual as part of their valid arrest.

Finally, it should be noted that private security officers can request that the local public officials obtain a search warrant based upon probable cause to believe that evidence will be found in a particular location or on a particular person. Such warrants are typically executed by public law enforcement officers although there are a few states which allow a private individual to be named as the executing official. A search conducted by a private citizen is still not subject to the exclusionary rule and the evidence seized could be used in a criminal trial against the individual searched. Tort responsibility for the person doing the illegal search can still be sued by the individual searched.

Questioning of Suspects

In most jurisdictions, a private security officer need not inform a suspect of his so-called Miranda rights prior to asking questions because the Fifth and Fourteenth Amendments to the Constitution apply only to governmental officials.

However, any statement must be freely given. Duress or forces used by a private person will render the statement involuntary. Such statements are inadmissible as a matter of evidentiary law because they are not reliable.

Use of Force

In determining the reasonableness of the force used by a private person, a reviewing court will look at the circumstances in light of the amount of force used, the seriousness of the crime prevented and the possibility of preventing the crime by other means. The use of excessive or unreasonable force could result in civil and criminal liability for assault and battery or even homicide charges if the victim dies.

Deadly force (also called lethal force) is force which is likely to kill or cause great bodily harm. Such force can be used to defend oneself or others from attack by someone using deadly force. In light of the considerations expressed by the United States Supreme Court in the case of Tennessee v. Garner, such force should not be used to stop a fleeing felon. As a general rule, deadly force can not be used to arrest unless there is also a threat to life involved.

Liability Issues

Civil liability is imposed for an intentional act or for a negligent act. In some situations, liability may be imposed without fault under a concept called strict liability.

Negligence is the failure of a person to exercise due diligence or reasonable care. Each of the following elements must be demonstrated by a preponderance of the evidence by the person bringing the lawsuit who is called the plaintiff:

1. Legal duty owed to the plaintiff by the defendant.
2. Failure to perform that duty.
3. Foreseeable injury caused by defendant's failure.
4. Damages suffered by the plaintiff.

Negligence actions have been successfully litigated against private security officers using one or more of the following theories: negligent use of force, negligent use of a motor vehicle, failure to protect, negligent hiring, negligent retention, failure to train, negligent supervision and negligent entrustment.

Where a duty has been imposed by law, one is judged by a reasonable man standard. The jury is instructed to consider whether the defendant's conduct was objectively reasonable under the circumstances of the case.

The other type of civil action is called an intentional tort. The plaintiff must prove by a preponderance of the evidence that the defendant acted with a particular mental state and with the knowledge that the result was substantially certain to follow. Example of the more common intentional torts are: false arrest or imprisonment, malicious prosecution, defamation, assault and battery, intentional invasion of privacy and the intentional infliction of mental distress.

An important element of any civil action is the proof of damage. Where a plaintiff has demonstrated a defendant's interference with a legally protected interest the court will award general damages to compensate the plaintiff for the loss suffered. Any special damages, for example medical expenses, may also be awarded. Where the injury resulted from the defendant's intent to harm, or from a willful and wanton disregard of the consequences of his action, punitive damages may be awarded. Punitive damages are designed to punish the defendant and deter such future conduct.

Basic skills are necessary for success in any field of study. Employers in the security/loss prevention field now realize that these basic skills include writing and legal analysis, as well as a broad range of practical skills that comprise the "nuts and bolts" of security.

Employees who are successfully sued in civil court for damages are individually responsible for paying the judgment awarded. Since few security employees have sufficient funds to satisfy large judgments, plaintiffs will attempt to bring into the lawsuit as many parties as possible. Not only will an employee be sued for misconduct, but usually the employer will be joined in the lawsuit under the doctrine of *respondeat superior*. The doctrine states that the employer is responsible for the acts of the employee when the act is committed within the scope of employment. The employer is liable under the doctrine even though the employer may be without fault and did not participate in the misconduct.

Employers are seeking well trained students as potential employees, who possess these skills, and therefore perform the tasks required by their employer within "legal limits." The knowledge of legal standards in security/loss prevention is essential for employees, so they can avoid liability for their employer. This skill is an invaluable attribute for an employee to possess.

Law classes are by their nature demanding; however, study of the law gives the foundation necessary to recognize potential conflicts or legal problems that must be dealt with in order to avoid legal liability and to prevent violation of the legal rights of others. Members of the security/loss prevention field should be familiar with legal issues and the applicable legal principles so they can regulate their own behavior on the job.

For example, in the area of public versus private law enforcement, when are you a security guard and when are you a public police officer? What difference does it make what they call you, as long as you do the job asked by your employer? A seemingly simple distinction between private and public law enforcement determines how you are to conduct yourself on the job and how your job performance will be legally evaluated. Private security officers are held to different legal standards than public police officers in how they can present themselves to the public, acceptable arrest procedures, techniques in search and seizure, and in use of deadly force.

It is essential to know the correct standards for both public and private law enforcement. If the wrong arrest standards are used in detaining an individual stealing from an employer the consequences may include the charges against the accused being dropped, new charges against the employee or the employer for abuses of the arrested individual's legal rights, and possibly a civil lawsuit against the employer for damages suffered by the individual during the erroneous arrest. To demonstrate the above scenario we can use the following shoplifting case.

An individual walks into the local Budget Store and proceeds to do some shopping. The security guard decides he does not like the individual's shopping techniques and decides to "shake him down" to determine if he is pocketing items without paying for them. The security guard approaches the individual and identifies himself as a police officer. A study of legal theory in civil security law would enable the student to realize that many errors have already been committed by the security guard. We can not do a crash course in security liability but we can put it in practical terms for you. A security guard can not stop an individual simply because he does not like his shopping techniques. The security guard's actions in stopping and detaining the individual are regulated and he must be careful how he performs his so-called "shake down." A private security guard must be careful not to misidentify himself as a police officer.

Can a police officer "moonlight" as a security guard for a private employer? A yes or no answer does not work for this question. Yes, police officers may work for private security as long as their police department allows moonlighting. Does he then function as a private person or as a police officer on the job for his private employer? This is an important legal distinction that must be understood if a police officer desires to supplement his income by working as a private security officer on his off-duty time.

Police officers are technically on duty 24 hours a day. Does his status as a police officer carry over to when he is privately paid to be a security officer? It makes a difference whether he is working as a police office or a private security officer to determine what it legally takes to show he has probable cause to arrest someone. Police are held to different legal standards in evaluating their conduct than those of a security officer who is considered a private citizen. Different standards for searches and seizures are applied in the private industry than for public police. If the correct legal standards are not used, the evidence seized by a police officer may be excluded as evidence at trial under the exclusionary rule. Is a security guard bound by the exclusionary rule? These questions are issues for a civil law class for the security field.

Basic knowledge in civil law for the security field can provide the tools necessary for the security employer and employee to avoid the repercussions that come from ignorant abuses. Are there regulations or licensing requirements for security personnel? In Illinois, for example, the security field is regulated by statute. There are basic personal and education requirements to be a licensed private detective and private security contractor. The code sets out the requirements necessary to be licensed and sanctions for specific violations of these requirements. Three years experience as a police officer or in private security out of the last five years is required for consideration for licensing, however, credit is given for education toward the experience required to be a private detective or security contractor. A degree from a four year college or university program gives two years experience out of the three years required. An associates degree from a two year community college program gives one year of experience out of the three that are required.

Specific training requirements exist by statute, training in the basic principles of law and liability, and firearm training when a firearm will be carried on the job. The statutes set out the material that must be covered in the training classes, how many hours of training classes are required and control of whom can teach the required classes.

Failure to comply with the licensing requirements is a class 4 felony in Illinois. To become a private investigator, it takes more than finding an office space and a degree from a college or university. There are specific requirements to qualify as an employee of a licensed detective or security contractor. The regulations, licensing and registration requirements are a basic topic covered by civil law courses in the security field, for whichever state that is pertinent.

Why is statutory control needed over the private security industry? It should be apparent that legal issues have more applicability to the security field than simply in a court room setting. Legal issues arise and need addressing in the daily work arena. Lack of knowledge of basic legal issues can be a hazard for the security employer, employees, and individuals they encounter on the job.

This article introduces some of the basic legal concepts that are relevant in the security field today. Students of the security field should immerse themselves in as much knowledge as is available to them through their college/university program in the area of legal issues. It is in the best interest of the security employer, the security employee and the citizens they come in contact with during their job performance, that today's students possess the analytical skills necessary to perform their job within the "legal limits." A student possessing these skills will be an invaluable asset to their potential employer.

CHAPTER 6

THE IMPORTANCE OF MANAGEMENT SKILLS IN THE SECURITY PROFESSION

Ron D. Davis
@1998 Ron D. Davis

A successful manager will need to develop certain skills. Among these are planning, motivation techniques, public speaking, personnel management, and budgeting. These areas will not only help in preparing the manager for the future but make them more effective in their current employment.

Quality security management is akin to a three dimensional triangle. One side of the triangle is quality management; another is quality concepts; and the last is quality security personnel. By balancing this three-dimensional triangle and, at the same time, interfacing within the organization as a whole, the security manager seeks to achieve quality security management.

If you know the way, the road from novice to security manager can be traveled in a reasonable time frame. This chapter will hopefully point you in the right direction and provide you with a rudimentary road map for the journey.

Because security management is a complex, multi-faceted field, I am using a straight forward "nuts and bolts" technique to discuss the essentials for operating in the current security environment.

The first four segments of this chapter encompasses the relationship between an effective manager and a quality security management environment.

The Changing Role of Security explores emerging management philosophies and the changing image of the security professional. The segment on **Planning -- One Key to Success,** reviews time management, strategic planning, and the inevitable adjustments that accompany any successful planning process.

The third section is rightfully entitled **People --The Real Key to Success.** The human element offers positive and negative feedback and determines the success of any quality security management program. **Financial Management** covers an area sometimes overlooked by a newcomer to the security profession. Dollars and sense to the security manager entails understanding budgets, anticipating hidden security costs, and methods of using the financial system to your advantage.

In the final section entitled **Preparing for the Challenge,** I offer practical information for students seeking career information about the security management field while still in the academic environment. I have emphasized this segment since it has more immediate value and attempts to road map an effective transition from student to security professional.

As a security professional with over 20 years experience in the field, I hope to assist you with that transition. In doing so, I am reminded of some advice a financial planner gave me some years back: "Never take financial advice from someone who makes less money than you do." This statement is applicable to most things in life, and certainly is the case in the security environment. Fortunately for the reader, a wealth of security experience and talent is evident throughout this book.

As a Director of Security for a five thousand employee Department of Defense (DoD) contractor, I had the daily opportunity to see the benefits derived from quality security practice and management. Quality management flows down from the top in any organization. Fortunately for me, upper management at Space Systems Division was always dedicated to quality security management principles. As I indicated earlier, keeping the triangle balanced is only part of the security manager's role. Working within the total organization is equally important.

Before I began my six year tenure in DoD security management, I spent twelve years as a Special Agent with the Federal Bureau of Investigation. Prior to my stint with the Bureau, I was an officer in the Marine Corps. For five years during the Vietnam era, I was a helicopter pilot and intelligence officer.

This cross section of military, law enforcement and industry-related experience has been an advantage in my current role. I recommend that security professionals seek as much cross-functional exposure as possible.

Perhaps one of the biggest advantages students have today is the opportunity to receive on-the-job training at companies such as General Dynamics through internship programs. General Dynamics' pioneer program with Western Illinois University is now in its eighth year. The program has offered the company a rare opportunity to assist students with the transition from college student to security professional. That experience has surfaced a few shortfalls in the academic process but it has also brought to our industry some wonderfully talented and motivated security managers of the future.

In the last section of this chapter I provide you with some thoughts for preparation, However, think of classes, in or out of your major, which might be of assistance; look at lectures or correspondence courses outside the university which might be valuable; and lastly look to part time and summer employment which will provide "hands-on" experience and look good on your resume.

The ultimate payoff for the security professional can be a rewarding and lucrative career in security management. There are managers and directors of security at all levels of the socioeconomic scale. The size and scope of a security management organization can vary from a one-person department in a small company to hundreds of employees in a major corporation.

The current salaries for managers range from approximately $20,000 to over $100,000 a year, depending on experience and responsibility level.

The contributions made by a security manager to his or her organization can be very fulfilling. Security professionals at some time during their career will make decisions that deal with fraud, sabotage, espionage, and other challenges that are not typical of most nine to five jobs in the marketplace. Opportunities are out there; the ball is in your court.

The Changing Role of Security

Quality security management is a derivation of Total Quality Management (TQM). This concept of TQM is sweeping the country and changing the way government and industry manage their resources. In a nutshell, Dr. W. Edward Deming is credited with transforming the Japanese economy through the TQM concept. Thanks to Deming's approach to management, Japan's economy went from an "also-ran" in the 1960's to a world-class leader in the 1980's. I am not going to cover Deming's 14 Points and what they mean, but you should certainly read his theories to recognize the direction security and other disciplines in American management are headed.

Adapting to change, such as the shift to TQM, is an important management function. If managers or security professionals cannot adapt to change, they should seek other career opportunities. Inspiring motivation in subordinates and peers requires that managers understand the forces that drive motivation. There are many good motivation and psychology courses you can take while in school. Don't get hung up in your major and forget the practical value of a liberal education.

One of the most important functions of a good security manager is to create a security environment where effective security practices can flourish and grow. This is accomplished by continuously improving all of our processes; encouraging upper management to set a positive example; developing new and better methods of communication; seeking professional approaches to security education; and building a true service organization. These are all positive examples of the changing role of security.

If security management is to be successful, we can no longer be thought of as the "company cops" or any of the other authoritarian catch phrases that have negative connotations. Security must be a service organization which supports the overall mission of the corporation but exercises the required controls. The role of the law enforcement officer is in a lengthy process of change along with the values and expectations of society. The security professional's role in industry has already changed, and the practitioners must change or suffer the consequences that accompany stagnation.

Important TQM phrases heard throughout American industry are "know who your customer is" and "strive for customer satisfaction." In the old days, we often lost sight of who the customer really was and what he or she actually wanted. In security, the "customer" is many people. They could be the employee on the factory floor, the Chief Executive Officer of the corporation, or the police officer contacting your facility. Taking time to recognize who the "customer" is and how to service that customer is another element in the changing role of security.

In this time of change, it is critical for both the security manager and the security professional to be guided by a strong code of ethics. As a security person, your ethical values and actions must be above reproach. Your credibility as a professional will be lost forever if on the one hand you try to administer the rules, while on the other, you demonstrate disregard for those same rules.

An interesting TQM driven change in management thinking is the inspection of the security processes themselves. This is an introspective look at how we can "work smarter" and/or streamline the normal administrative functions. At the forefront of the improvement of the processes is the computerization of the security functions.

In the past few years, many progressive companies have computerized document control, security briefing schedules, visitor control, and contract administration. There are additional savings to be realized and efficiency to be gained with innovative application of computers. Immediately, and for the long term, emerging security professionals must be more than computer literate, they must become computer experts. My advice is for students to take all the computer classes they can fit into their schedules.

Lastly, a new and interesting change is the emergence of a new discipline known as System Security Engineering or System Security Management. This new pro-active approach utilizes engineering principles and mathematical models to design cost efficient security into a system before it is built. The word system is used in the broadest generic sense and could refer to a simple locking device, building or an entire factory complex.

Planning -- One Key to Success

For you personally, or for the employee reporting to a security manager, time management is one of the critical factors in planning and implementation.

The best way I have found to overcome the ever-present problem of over scheduling, changing priorities, and meeting objectives is through the use of a planner/diary system. After trying a number of systems, I find the DAY-TIMER system to be the best for me.

The DAY-TIMER comes in various sizes and shapes intended to meet an individual's needs. My DAY-TIMER fits in my suit pocket. It contains two pages per day to plan the current and following month and a separate schedule of two pages per month for the next couple of years. the system uses a 5-in-1 page layout which allows you to organize entries into five key categories: 1) Appointments; 2) To Be Done Today; 3) Advance Reminders; 4) Work Diary/ Time Log, and 5) Expense Record.

These seem to be my five key categories as well. As a manager, getting to appointments on time is essential and the "To Do" section allows me to prioritize my responsibilities. The

Work Diary serves as a repository for recording all transactions which should be retained for future reference. A good system will cost approximately $25 to $50 to get started and another $15 per year to maintain.

After acquiring a DAY-TIMER or similar device, I recommend that you devote 15 minutes each morning to planning. You can organize your day by reviewing what was accomplished, what didn't get done, and what new things surfaced necessitating new priorities. The more difficult, but equally important task, is strategic planning. An effective manager should spend a significant portion of his or her planning time looking one, three, five or seven years into the future in order to use time more productively.

A part of the long range plan or strategic planning process is anticipating problems. As a manager and, to a lesser extent, as a new security practitioner, you must examine your future requirements for personnel, facilities, budgets, and transitions into new ventures or techniques. Under the "all of us is smarter than one of us" theory, it is often advantageous to use a team approach to solving these kinds of problems. The final step is to schedule reviews periodically to see if your planning and implementation are working as anticipated.

A successful CEO recently attributed his success to anticipation, planning, follow-up, finding root causes, and over killing problems. It is not always easy to apply these points to your own situation, but it provides a good framework for security or any other management function. Planning, when applied to real world situations always evolves into replanning and adjusting to compensate for unanticipated variables.

The goal of planning is a quality security product. Phrased another way, to achieve a quality product, we must often look to the future and be innovative. In security, this must include planning for computerization, robotics, advanced communications, bio-metrics and other new products.

Break down the planning process into manageable segments when dealing with major projects or solving complex problems; otherwise they may become overwhelming. After identifying these sub-sets, the task then becomes one of establishing realistic and achievable goals to accomplish the individual objectives. As the whole is the sum of its parts, the overall project or problem will take care of itself.

People --The Real Key to Success

People are the most important ingredient in any organization. They are also the most difficult ingredient to manage. Personnel is always the critical consideration in dealing with all of the issues being addressed here; i.e., change, problem solving, planning, or establishing budgets.

For your long-range thinking, a manager must consider all of the issues addressed in this section to be effective. The student, in anticipation of becoming a security professional, should review the substance and logic of the following points and tailor his or her personal performance accordingly.

Always hire the best possible people to work for you. A manager who is insecure or threatened by bright new employees will seldom be successful. Good people only make a good manager look better. A logical corollary to the best person rule is to hire the right person for a given job. The world's finest electronics countermeasure person is probably not the right person to fill a requisition for a personnel security administrator. A good manager thrives for a balance of experience, gender, skills, age, and growth potential.

Knowing who you are hiring (or who you are going to work for) is an essential part of the security management function. I am a strong advocate of background investigations, utilizing personal contacts or networking to assess a candidate. Depending on the job level and experience required, the "track record" of the potential employee is essential to a security manager. Drug usage or arrests can be a stumbling block for entry into the security profession. General Dynamics and many other corporations require pre-employment drug screening. Any non-prescription drugs in your system at the time of testing will automatically eliminate you as a job candidate. Although not intended to minimize the seriousness of drugs, many companies recognize that some students have made mistakes and used drugs on an experimental basis. This type of situation is normally not an immediate disqualifier. Usually these cases are reviewed on an individual basis. Recency and frequency of use are the key discriminators in the decision process where drugs are concerned.

Although prior arrest for minor infractions will probably not eliminate a person who has other strong attributes, it may make them less competitive during the selection process.

The last and perhaps hardest factor to judge is how a candidate fits in with the team as a whole. Typically, an organization reflects the management style of its leader; therefore, managers tend to hire individuals reflective of themselves. Put another way, the people a manager attracts often reflect the manager's leadership and style. Certainly, no one wants to work for a tyrant, unethical, or unpredictable boss. "Bad chemistry" in the initial interview should be a significant warning sign to either party.

There are several basic concepts which any good manager endorses. The application of these concepts should be used as a yard stick to judge the effectiveness of that manager. A manager must provide leadership. A manager should also treat everyone with respect and dignity. He or she should optimize the education, skills and abilities of the staff and insure everyone receives adequate compensation and rewards. Effective training should be provided to encourage growth. A manager must know the staff and be sensitive to its welfare.

The development of subordinates must be an ongoing process. This is addressed in a variety of ways. The development process is enhanced if the manager doesn't just allow the staff to bring problems to his or her attention, but also requires solutions (or at least options) to be provided.

A technique which has proved effective within the General Dynamics organization is cross-functional training and rotation of security personnel. Designed for less experienced individuals interested in gaining additional skills, General Dynamics attempts to rotate individuals who have been in their specific job for 18 to 24 months.

Such is the case with former WIU interns Dave Walters and Todd Dolezal. Walters joined the Space Systems security staff as a WIU Intern in 1985 and was subsequently hired as a Classified Document Control Administrator. Over an 18-month period, Walters became proficient in all aspects of document control and related investigations.

When Dolezal completed his internship and was offered a position on the staff in 1988, he was given responsibility for document control. Rather than taking the easy route and keeping Walters in document control while training Dolezal for something new, Walters was provided the opportunity to transition into Physical Security and Automated Information Systems.

The cycle continued as Walters replaced a more experienced administrator who was promoted to a management position. Dolezal, with a year's experience in document control was eventually moved into security education to complete a cross-functional training cycle. This is a situation where everyone is a winner. The individuals can gain additional skills, and the department benefits from its cross-trained personnel.

I believe there are several ways to accomplish any given task and still offer employees latitude in which to get the job done, thus providing job satisfaction and personal growth. The problem solving approach versus the proscribed procedure approach encourages faster learning and often streamlines the process. While giving an employee the freedom to accomplish a task, he or she becomes responsible for the consequences of his or her actions. This provides further job satisfaction for the employee who is capable and a self-starter.

Positive role models are also an important product for employee development. A good manager demonstrates the leadership skills on a daily basis that he or she wants to instill in subordinates. Managers must make sound and timely decisions that are impartial to the staff. The manager should expect imagination and innovation from the staff. He or she must communicate effectively and keep everyone informed. The entire staff should attend a weekly meeting designed to foster two-way communication.

Job descriptions and responsibilities must be clear, concise, and available to everyone. There must be adequate attention focused on subordinates' physical and psychological well being. Remember, some stress is positive; too much is lethal.

A quality manager is quick to recognize and credit the accomplishments of subordinates. Conversely, unwarranted blame should never be attributed to a subordinate. One of the most damaging mistakes a manager can make is to take credit for work done by others, or to blame others for the manager's mistakes.

Lastly, a good manager encourages staff members to pursue good promotional opportunities when and if they arise. If a manager does not allow his or her quality people to advance, it is the beginning of the end. Good people with the drive and ability to progress will avoid working for that manager.

Financial Management

For many security managers, the budget process and related financial matters are among the less desirable aspects of the job. This is typically due to a lack of experience in finance. Since finance will always be a critical part of the management function and can be used to your advantage, wise students should attempt to prepare themselves while still in school.

Security is labor intensive in relation to many other functions within the company. Guard costs normally make up a significant share of the security budget, and they are a recurring (annual) cost. There are some hidden costs which must be understood to properly budget or estimate.

A simple but often overlooked concern when estimating costs is targeting the number of guards required for a given task. It is generally accepted among security professionals that to "man" a one-person post for 24 hours per day, 7 days a week, you must hire five people. That figure takes into account three shifts on weekdays, vacations, holidays, and during sick time.

When those five people are hired, you cannot just multiply their salaries by 5. Instead, you must add 35-40 percent for benefits, training and other overhead costs. The recurring cost of human assets at a guard post can be substantial. This can be mitigated by using guards to accomplish other tasks in addition to their primary responsibility.

The subject of guard budgets always brings up the basic issue of Contract versus Proprietary guards, and which offers the best coverage. In my opinion, there is no right answer, because the need is controlled by the particular situation. General Dynamics uses almost an equal number of contract and proprietary guards. With contract guards, you don't typically pay for benefits but you pay the contract guard company profit and overhead for their services.

Although contract guards are often less expensive to hire, they tend to be more transient and less loyal to their employer.

There are a number of innovative ways to use contract services as a supplement to an organization's established resources. The use of contract personnel for badging services and investigations are two such possibilities.

Anytime an employer is dealing with contract guards or other subcontractors, the issue of ethics or the perception of unethical activity is crucial. I can't emphasize enough how important it is for the security practitioner to demonstrate actions that are always beyond reproach. Remember, perception is reality in the minds of most people.

The budget for the security department should be challenging, but realistic. In other words, don't ask for more than you need, but do expect enough to meet your obligations and requirements. My formula for the optimal budget is one that estimates a very accurate or "tight" budget and then adds a management reserve of 10 to 15 percent to cover additional expenses or unanticipated overtime. It is important to list what the vulnerabilities are, what will be needed to protect your assets and the costs involved.

The last valuable lesson in financial management is to learn to use the system. All organizations have a certain amount of bureaucracy which can honestly be used as an advantage. For example, the month of the year an employee is promoted can have a bearing on whether or not that employee can also receive a meritorious pay increase for that year. That knowledge is important if you are concerned with keeping your salaries competitive with the rest of the industry. An effective manager must know when promotions are given and the lead time required.

In any company you must constantly be alert to justify your budget requirements, know where the money will come from, know if you can share cost with another department and if there are any other beneficiaries of the employment. Detail, accuracy, and credibility are essential to selling your budget needs. "Specificity is golden," sayeth the bean counters.

Preparing for the Challenge

As I explained earlier in the chapter, this final section is the "nuts and bolts" of quality security management. I address the immediate needs and requirements of a student working toward a degree in security. You will notice some redundancy and some new material. In all cases, it is hoped that the reader is able to learn which additional academic courses and/or opportunities would enhance his or her career growth.

First and foremost, a solid academic foundation is needed. Courses in English, English composition and journalism build solid writing skills. Speech classes that involve the interviewing process, public speaking, debating, and drama develop effective verbal skills.

Management classes in statistics, finance, personnel management, accounting, psychology, labor relations, and information systems are valuable academic choices also.

Classes in the legal discipline are also helpful to a security professional. Courses in civil and criminal law will enhance a student's ability to meet new challenges.

Exposure to computers is a must in today's business world. Every student should take theoretical and practical application computer courses.

Work for exemplary grades. Good jobs go to good students. Your track record is a critical discriminator for job selection. Therefore, when coming from an academic environment, an employer uses grades as a primary track record for considering you as a job candidate.

Remember your resume is enhanced by extracurricular activities in and out of the school environment. Choose activities that demonstrate your drive, motivation, intelligence, persistence and maturity.

Attempt to establish a personal style that demonstrates integrity, ethical behavior and honesty, which are attributes expected from any professional security practitioner. Although most security managers won't expect extensive on-the-job experience, they will look for bright, mature and motivated individuals who have demonstrated strong character and integrity.

Through personal contacts, academic contacts, or professional associations such as the American Society for Industrial Security (ASIS), a student can meet active security practitioners and learn about different organizations and available opportunities.

Through these same sources, a student can obtain some "hands-on" law enforcement and become familiar with peace officers. Although this chapter is dedicated to private sector security, many opportunities are available through federal and local law enforcement.

As a student, you should take advantage of the opportunity to join security associations such as ASIS or law enforcement auxiliary groups. When attending meetings and functions, students can make contacts and learn more about the profession.

With an ASIS membership, the student receives the monthly magazine entitled *Security Management*. This magazine is an additional benefit for a newcomer to the field, because it reflects the current thinking on security issues by security practitioners.

Read security texts in your area of interest, specifically outside your course work. Additional input from other sources provides different perspectives on the subject. Butterworth Publications are worth looking into.

Develop your own "nuts and bolts" security skills in your spare time. These might include locksmithing, fingerprinting, alarm installation and maintenance, photography, computer programming, electronic countermeasures, guard services, and architectural security.

When competing with other recent graduates for jobs in the security field, a student with specific security related skills may have a distinct advantage over someone with generic skills. Although most security managers understand that a training period is necessary when a student comes to the organization, they will logically view the candidate's practical experience as an immediate value to the security department.

Don't underestimate the value of "people skills" through public relations classes, negotiation training, community service, retail sales, and self improvement classes. Verbal skill and appearance during the screening process often are considered as deciding factors between close job candidates.

As part of that process, think about ways to enhance your physical image. Dressing for success is more than a casual phrase. Exterior image also extends to neatness in hairstyle, clean nails and weight management.

During an interview, feel free to ask questions. Be sure, however, you have done your homework. Contrary to popular legend, there is such a thing as a dumb question.

More important to the newcomer is finding a part-time job, internship, or volunteer position within the security industry. Any security experience will assist a student when competing for a job after graduation.

Screen all opportunities to learn the best direction toward your career path. Obviously, if you want to go into Industrial Security, you should attempt to find an internship in industry, not with a police agency.

If you elect to do an internship, line up a quality internship program in your area of interest. Don't look at it as just one more class or semester. Your selection of an internship and your performance while in that internship may be the single most influential decision in determining your destiny.

Also, look at that agency's history of placing students in good positions following the internship or part-time job. Definitely look for an internship in an organization with high placement statistics.

Whether it's in an internship or a new job, always look for quality security management. If you are fortunate enough to find a quality security management program utilizing quality concepts, the road to becoming a quality security professional will be short.

CHAPTER 7

RISKY BUSINESS: HIRING, RETAINING, AND FIRING EMPLOYEES

J. Gayle Mericle, Ph.D.
Kenneth A. Clontz, Ph.D.
Department of Law Enforcement
and Justice Administration
Western Illinois University

There is no component more valuable or potentially dangerous to a company than its employees. While this statement is hardly news, it bears repeating as a reminder to all involved in the hiring process that careful, well-researched employing is no longer a stated ideal, but a necessity. A haphazard approach to recruiting, selecting, testing and interviewing provides an open door for civil litigation. Additionally, an ill-considered hire can result in a number of types of losses: time, money, information, morale, and in these uncertain times, even life itself. The responsibility for this expanded version of "loss prevention" falls at least in part on the shoulders of security.

Often the relationship between Human Resource managers and security managers becomes strained because each views the hiring of personnel from differing perspectives. Security prefers to focus on finding ethical, stable employees, while those seeking personnel to fill company vacancies are usually interested in getting qualified, competent people for positions. In these increasingly technical times, applicants with the valuable requisite skills sought by employers can become rare commodities. There can be a strong temptation for those in Human Resources to take short cuts in the hiring process, or even skip some steps all together to sign the skilled worker.

Security directors and supervisors share the daunting task of weeding out unsuitable personnel while simultaneously avoiding the quagmire of the Equal Employment Opportunity Commission (EEOC) and other Federal regulatory guidelines and meeting the mandates of their company's Human Resource office. This chapter introduces readers to what is required in pursuing legal employment practices as outlined in federal statutes, while highlighting potential problems and pitfalls. (Every employer needs to consult his or her state laws regarding employment as these sometimes differ from the federal guidelines.) As in many other endeavors, it will soon become clear that prior planning and a commitment to follow through are keys to success.

FEDERAL ANTI-DISCRIMINATORY LAWS

Anti-discriminatory laws at both the state and federal level apply to every stage of the hiring process. These regulations must be taken into consideration when the employer is preparing the job description, writing ads, conducting interviews, making decisions on who to hire, setting salaries and job benefits, promoting employees and terminating them. Employment practices are deemed illegal whenever the state and/or federal courts have decided that a characteristic, such as gender, has no legitimate relationship to an employment decision. This in no way means the courts are dictating who a company or business hires. All it does is insure that employers make decisions about every phase of employment based on the employees' skills, experience, performance, and reliability. Employers remain free to exercise their discretion in hiring, promoting, disciplining, and firing employees as long as their decisions are logically based on valid business related factors. Violations only occur when employers treat individuals or groups differently for reasons that the legislators or judges have established as not serving a legal business purpose (Steingold, 1997).

While covering each of the laws prohibiting discrimination in-depth is outside the scope of this work, what follows is a synopsis of the legislation that impacts most heavily on employment practices.

Title VII of the Civil Rights Act states employers cannot use race, color, religion, gender, or national origin as the basis for decisions on hiring, promotions, dismissals, work assignments, leaves of absence- or just about any other facet of the working relationship. (Sexual Harassment is not specifically mentioned under Title VII, but is now considered included here as an illegal variety of gender discrimination) Title VII applies to any business employing 15 or more people, either full time or part-time. In most cases, state laws have similar provisions against discrimination, and cover employers with fewer employees.

Title VII is one of the best known federal attempts to prohibit discrimination, but it is far from the only such legislation.

The Americans With Disabilities Act (ADA) makes hiring and employment decisions illegal if they discriminate against anyone because of a disability. If a person is qualified to do the work, or could do it once reasonable accommodations are made, then the employer must treat that person the same as all other applicants and employees.

The Age Discrimination in Employment Act (ADEA) prohibits discrimination against older workers. Discrimination in employee benefit programs based on the employee's age is outlawed under the **Older Workers Benefit Protection Act**. Protections provided under both these laws is extended to workers who are 40 years or older.

The Pregnancy Discrimination Act makes it illegal to discriminate against pregnant women in any aspect of employment because of pregnancy, childbirth, or related medical conditions.

The Equal Pay Act outlaws discrimination in wages on the basis of gender.

The National Labor Relations Act makes it illegal to discriminate against employees because they do or do not belong to a labor union.

The Immigration Reform and Control Act prohibits discrimination based on whether or not a person is a citizen of the United States.

The Polygraph Protection Act forbids the use of polygraphs and voice print devices except in cases of specified exceptions.

Though patently not an anti-discriminatory law, one further piece of federal legislation needs to be mentioned here: the **Occupational Safety and Health Act (OSHA)** is a comprehensive law designed to reduce workplace hazards and improve safety and health programs for workers. Its requirements broadly mandate that employers provide a workplace free of physical dangers.

DEVELOPING THE JOB DESCRIPTION

Security managers and personnel often discover that their company has either few or no written job descriptions, or the existing ones have little to do with the current jobs actually being performed by workers. Whether one needs to prepare the description from scratch or review an existing position's definition, creating or updating job descriptions is an essential step in making a good hire. Keep in mind that a well-thought out description of functions and duties expected of the new employee gives employers a guide by which to explain the job to applicants. It also assists in developing a list of criteria the successful candidate needs to meet. Once the new employee is selected, the job description provides him or her with a direction and basis from which to start, while providing supervisors with a tool for measurement of performance (Dorbrish, Wolff, and Zevnik, 1984; Wendover, 1995). Additionally, time spent putting together a concise and complete job description to fit current employment needs saves time and effort in the long run by providing a preliminary sieve through which to screen applicants.

Job descriptions can vary dramatically in style, but should share certain characteristics. An ideal job description takes the form of a precise document identifying factually the work functions the employee is expected to perform and the responsibility included in the job. This description is based on the nature of the work required rather than the work being performed by the individual currently occupying the position.

So how do we get there from a standing start? Once it is determined that a position, proposed or existing, is necessary, the first step toward creating the job description is conducting a job analysis. This does not have to entail an involved or convoluted process, nor should it be allowed to develop into a perceived threatening procedure for employees working in the position to be audited. Clear, definite communication about why the job is being "inspected" is needed to shortstop rumors and employee fears. Welcome his or her input, but avoid having the person performing the job under consideration do the analysis or write the job description. Human nature tends to prompt individuals into exaggerating their responsibilities and importance (Wendover, 1995). So, for example, when Security conducts a job analysis, it should be the director of Security who uses the data gathered about the work functions and writes the job description.

A job audit form provides a good basis for building the job analysis. It needs to ask specific listings of both major and minor duties, who someone in the position is supervised by, the number of employees the position holder supervises, what training and education are required, what certificates and licenses are required, what experience is required (identifying specific skills), physical requirements, and any on the job hazards/working conditions. Each job audit form is to be signed by the person making the input. Once the audits are complete, the person with the responsibility for writing the job description should review them and select out the true functional requirements for the position. If the job description is being written for a newly proposed job, then asking for input from other employees about what the position should entail is still a good option. When actually creating the description, however, pare down the "wish list" to realistically reflect what a person can achieve in the job's time frame.

Before putting together the job description, one other factor must be considered. If the job to be advertised legitimately requires that a certain gender, nationality, religion, or other characteristic is necessary to perform the job, then the employer may state this restriction in the ad. The requirement for a factor which would ordinarily appear to be discriminatory must be a bona fide occupational qualification (BFOQ). For example, if a security guard will be required to invade personal privacy by searching female employees, then a legitimate BFOQ would be that the applicants should be female. What is not permissible is any assumption that excludes potential applicants due to gender. Advertising for a "stockman" because the position requires heavy lifting is illegal. Gender in this case is not a BFOQ. The job description used in the ad should read "individuals hired should be able to lift 80 pounds."

Once armed with the information from the job analysis, the writing of the description can begin. A general format to follow when documenting the position needs begins with the job title, the organizational unit, and a statement of accountability. Next comes a job summary, with a listing of duties and responsibilities. This is not the place in the job description to skimp on words. "Is responsible for safety and security of products and personnel" is simply not adequate. If the employee is expected to do it, put it in writing. Include what is to be done, why it is to be done, when it is to done if that is not self-evident, and how the function is to be performed. Anything less makes for a useless job description. Once these expected work activities are clarified, continue by specifying the relationships or interactions between this job and others in the company. Finally indicate who prepared the job description, who approved it, and the date of preparation. Dating the work makes it easier to decide how current the job description information is (Dobrish et al., 1984; Steingold, 1997).

Whoever has the overall responsibility for administering job descriptions is expected to impose a uniformity of styles and format in the descriptions before they are published. This remains true even when a number of people from different parts of the organization are involved in preparing them. This person checks to make sure the format guidelines are met and works to insure clarity in all the job descriptions used by her or his employer.

Once the job description is formalized, advertising for the position begins. Just as in the job description, remember to consider the legal guidelines. Phrasing and even unintentional nuances appearing in an ad can be used as evidence that the company discriminates against applicants of a certain gender, age, or marital status (Steingold, 1997). Even if it seems initially awkward, use neutral words in the ad. For instance, one no longer advertises for a waiter or waitress, one seeks wait staff. A "handyman" is also out, but everyone can use a General Repair person.

One simple way of meeting legal requirements is to obstinately stick to the job skills needed and the position's basic responsibilities when writing the ad. Once these are satisfactorily described, have several people proofread the ad for any errors or biased language. Clear language about what is expected of the potential employee allows companies to legitimately reject applicants who do not have the necessary credentials, skills, or abilities to perform the job tasks. Going to the extra trouble to tailor the job ad now may save the company extensive and expensive trouble later.

Finding the best person for the job means advertising in candidate pools that should contain qualified people. Obviously, what a company is willing to spend on advertising a job is in part determined by the type of opening to be filled, but the main focus should be on finding that best person for the job. A usual avenue for advertising for employees is in newspaper classified ads in cities where the position will be staffed. A good, upbeat ad will be important for attracting the attention of qualified job seekers (Dobrish et al., 1984). It is crucial that the ad is strictly accurate in portraying the job advertised, giving the complete job description and salary range. This can make the difference between getting mediocre applicants that are "sort of" what the firm is looking for, and drawing great applicants that truly fit the job requirements.

Newspaper classified sections are not the only way to get the employee search message out. Trade publications and journals are excellent places to advertise, reaching candidates that are already in or familiar with the company's industry. Radio and television may or may not be too costly for the ad campaign, but there is no excuse for not using the Internet to circulate information about the job. Actively recruiting at job fairs, industry conferences and conventions, and seminars related to the work not only can be very productive, but have the added advantage of allowing a face to face meeting with potential employees before formal interviews are conducted. And of course, do not overlook recruiting new workers by asking current full-time employees if any of their friends or acquaintances fit the job search parameters.

The next logical step in the employment procedure is to have all persons responding to the ad to fill out a formal application. A well-drafted application form attempts to elicit information necessary to make a preliminary determination about whether or not the applicant meets the job description requirements (Siegel and Bryant, 1997). But here too, there can be pitfalls. Review any existing application forms and make sure that they do not ask for data that is not job-related. Problems crop up when an employer either knowingly or unwittingly asks questions that any of the federal employment laws have deemed illegal. Table 1 provides examples of questions that can and cannot be asked on the job application form, during the interviewing process, and while conducting the background investigation.

Table 1

Examples of Acceptable and Unacceptable Inquiries for Pre-employment Testing

Subject	Unacceptable Inquiries	Acceptable Inquiries
Address or Duration of Residence	Do you own or rent your home?	What is your place of residence? How long have you resided in this state or city?
Age	How old are you? What is your birth date? What are your children's ages? Dates of attendance or completion of elementary or high school.	Are you over 18 years of age or older? If hired can you show proof of age? If under 18, can you after employment submit a work permit?
Arrest and Convictions Records	Have you ever been arrested? Do you currently have any felony charges pending against you? Have you ever been charged with a crime?	Have you been convicted of a crime? Is so, give details.
Birthplace, Citizenship	Of what country are you a citizen? Are you naturalized or a native-born citizen? What date did you acquire citizenship? Do you plan to become a citizen of the U.S.? Are your parents or spouse naturalized or native-born United States citizens?	Are you authorized to work in the United States? Can you, after employment, submit verification of your legal right to work in the United States? or statement that such proof may be required after employment.

66

Subject	Unacceptable Inquiries	Acceptable Inquiries
	What date did your parents or spouse acquire United States citizenship?	
Disability	What is your corrected vision? Have you ever been unable to cope with job related stress? Do you have a disability that would interfere with your ability to perform the job? When will your broken leg heal? Can you stand? Questions regarding receipt of Workers Compensation	Do you have 20/20 corrected vision? How well can you handle stress? How did you break you leg? Can you stand for 5 hours? Can you walk 20 miles in one day? Can you meet the attendance requirements of this job?
Discharge from Military Service	Did you serve in the armed forces of another country? Did you receive a discharge that was less than honorable?	Have you ever been a member of the United States armed services or in a state militia? If so, what branch? If so, explain your experience in relation to the position for which your are applying. Did you receive a dishonorable discharge? (Inquiries regarding military service should be accompanied by a statement that a dishonorable discharge is not an absolute bar to employment and that other factors will affect the final decision)
Education		What private or public schools did you attend?

Subject	Unacceptable Inquiries	Acceptable Inquiries
		Describe your academic, vocational or professional education as it related to this position
English Language Skills	What is your native language? How did you acquire your foreign language skill?	What foreign language do you read, write, and/or speak fluently?
Experience		Inquiries include those regarding work experience
Marital Status, Number of Children, Child Care, Sex	Are you married? single? divorced? separated? What are the ages of your children? What is your spouse's name? What is your sexual preference? What is your spouse's salary? What are your child care plans? Whom can we contact in case of emergency? (This question can be asked after a person has been hired) Do you wish to be addressed as Miss? Mrs.? Ms.? Questions regarding pregnancy, child bearing, or birth control.	Information such as this which is required for tax, insurance, or social security purposes may be obtained after hiring. Lawful inquiries include those regarding one's ability to travel if the job required it. However, all applicants must be asked the same question.
Notice in Case of Emergency	Name and address of person to be notified in case of	Name and address of person to be notified in case of

Subject	Unacceptable Inquiries	Acceptable Inquiries
	accident or emergency (Information obtained after the applicant has been hired)	accident or emergency. Name and address of a relative or spouse to be notified in case of accident or emergency.
Name	Please state your maiden name. If you have worked under another name, state that name and dates.	Have you ever worked for this company under a different name? Is additional information relative to change of name, use of an assumed name or nickname necessary to enable a check on your work record? If yes, explain.
Organizations, Activities	List all clubs, societies, and lodges to which you belong.	Please state your membership in any organization(s) which you feel is/are relevant to your ability to perform this job.
Physical Description, Photograph	Questions as to applicant's height and weight Require applicant to affix a photograph to application Request applicant at his or her option to submit a photograph Require a photograph after interview but before employment Inquiries include those that are not related to job requirements	Any questions that have an impact on one's ability to perform the job requirements. Statement that photograph may be required after employment
Race, Color, Religion,, or National Origin	Questions as to applicant's race or color.	Statement by employer of regular days, hours, or shifts to be worked

Subject	Unacceptable Inquiries	Acceptable Inquiries
	Questions regarding applicant's complexion or color of skin, eyes, hair Questions regarding applicant's religion Questions regarding religious days observed Does your religion prevent you from working weekends or holidays? Questions as to nationality, lineage, ancestry, national origin, descent, or parentage of applicant, applicant's parents, or spouse.	
References	Questions of applicant's former employers or acquaintances which elicit information specifying the applicant's race, color, religious creed, national origin, ancestry, physical handicap, medical conditions, marital status, age, or sex	By whom were you referred for a position here? Names of persons willing to provide professional and or character references for applicant.

No application form is complete without a section obtaining written consent by the applicant to conduct a background investigation and a reference check. Having the individual's signature on the application form okaying the action makes it extremely difficult for the person to make valid invasion of privacy claims. It also shortstops complaints that the potential employee did not know that his or her background would be researched.

Another recommended section requiring the applicant's signature is one in which the job candidate verifies that the information he or she provides on the application is true, complete, and correct. It should also clearly state that any false or incomplete statements made by the applicant will be grounds for immediate employment termination. This is not an idle threat. Courts have deemed applicant fraud to be a serious enough breach of acceptable conduct to warrant the dismissal of the offending employee. The potential employee's signature next to a verification statement cancels out any defense of ignorance on the part of the applicant.

One last cautionary remark. Application fraud is a real problem in today's workforce. To safeguard against dishonest applicants having someone else fill out the form for them, it is a wise practice to have all job seekers fill out the application on company premises where security can keep an eye on them. This reduces the risk of the application form becoming an exercise in group or creative writing.

Once applications and resumes are received, the real initial task of screening begins. Both documents should be examined for general appearance. This is not a trivial point, nor is it nit-picking. This person has submitted paperwork on which his or her livelihood depends. A sloppy application and/or resume speaks volumes about the applicant.

Besides appearance, check for spelling errors, use of grammar, and correct use of tense. Writing ability is a critical skill for security personnel. If an applicant does not display proper English and grammar on forms and documents that he or she knows will be carefully reviewed, it is unlikely that person will miraculously improve when producing daily reports.

Take special note of the applicant's educational credentials, stated experience, and the chronology of previous employment. While all these avenues of information are subject to checking during the background investigation, they are important now in determining whether or not the applicant is qualified for the position advertised. If the applicant clearly does not meet the announced requisites for the job, immediately cull his or her application from the ones to be considered and notify the individual that he or she are not qualified for the current opening. This saves time for both the application reviewer and the unqualified applicant. The applicant knows to continue the job search while the reviewer only spends time on those applicants meeting the employment criteria.

EMPLOYMENT TESTING

Employment testing is a controversial issue. The mere mention of personnel testing as a part of the hiring process elicits either a response or challenge. Some people will cite experiences that show testing to be ineffective and those who can make claims of great decisions based on its output (Mali, 1986; Wendover, 1995). The decision to test, whether physically or psychologically, is totally up to individual employers, except for companies regulated by Department of Defense (DOT), Department of Transportation (DOT), and the Nuclear Regulatory commission regulations (Joel, 1996; Wendover, 1995). The downside of testing is it is expensive, time consuming, and if improperly used may lead to litigation. However, pre-employment screening of potential employees is an accurate indicator in certain situations (Mali, 1986; Wendover, 1995).

According to a 1990 American Management Association survey of companies using workplace testing, 45% were testing for job competency, 36% of the companies were testing for basic skills, and 10% were testing using paper and pencil integrity tests. (Wendover, 1995). Today pre-employment testing can be divided into two major categories: psychological screening and physical screening.

Psychological Testing

The psychological category consists of skill-based competence, aptitude testing, and honesty testing, while the physical screening may include actual medical examinations, drug and alcohol screening, and testing for Acquired Immune Deficiency Syndrome (AIDS) (Steingold, 1997; Wendover, 1995).

Skill-based Testing

Skill-based tests are designed to measure what people already know how to do instead of what they are suited to do (Dobrish et al., 1984; Doele and Dukes, 1986; Jessup, 1970; Steingold, 1997). Applicants' perceptions of what they can accomplish are often at odds with their "true" ability. Testing job skills and knowledge about the job to verify applicants' actual skill level is important (Dobrish et al., 1984; Steingold, 1997).

Skill-based testing takes the form of either a written test, a practical test, or a combination of the two. Often the "written" test requires no writing by the applicant. Instead, these tests use objective-type questions with multiple-choice answers. The advantage of this type of testings is that items can be marked simply and accurately, where similar questions requiring a written answer could be marked right or wrong depending on the examiner (Dobrish et al., 1984; Jessup, 1970).

While "written" tests can adequately measure knowledge, assessment of skills requires a demonstration. This demonstration normally means performing the actual job skill. Performance of a skill usually involves some motor activity of the body. Still, words can be used to cover other behaviors such as managerial skills, social skills, or verbal skills, where situations rather than things are handled (Jessup, 1970).

Employers benefit from skill testing in two ways. First, candidates can be ranked from "most qualified" to "least qualified" using predetermined criteria. Second, these tests can uncover training needs and help a company develop a better training program (Dobrish, Wolff, and Zevnik, 1984). Remember to avoid discriminating against applicants, be sure that the company's selected tests measure actual skills needed to do the job. Tests reflecting impaired mental, sensory, manual, or speaking skills will violate the Americans with Disabilities Act (ADA) unless these skills are genuinely related to the job duties (Steingold, 1997).

Aptitude Tests

Aptitude testing measures a person's capacity to learn required job skills (Dobrish et al., 1984) or to probe the applicants' psyche (Steingold, 1997). These types of tests are going out of fashion for a number of reasons. First, these multiple-choice tests may reflect test-taking ability rather than actual job skills which may discriminate against minority applicants. Second, employers may invade an applicant's privacy. Finally, the ADA sets special requirements when testing people who have impaired skills. Tests must be designed so that applicants do not have to use their impaired skills unless they are required for the job (Steingold, 1997). If a person is hearing impaired and answering the telephone is a function of the job, then this can be used as a criteria in testing. However, if the person will be writing reports, then tests dealing with his or her ability to talk on the telephone are illegal under the ADA.

Honesty Tests

In 1988, the National Business Crime Information Network reported losses of more than $200 billion in cash and merchandise theft which employees committed. According to the Department of Justice, insider theft is growing at an annual rate of 15% (Wendover, 1995). In an attempt to reduce the problem of employee theft, employers have turned to honesty tests. Honesty tests, integrity tests, and lie detection tests all refer to the same concept which is to determine whether the applicant or employee is telling the truth (Fischer and Green, 1998; Wendover, 1995). This section focuses on the three major categories: (a) the Personal Security Inventory, (b) the Psychological Stress Evaluator, and (c) the polygraph or "lie detector" test (Fischer and Green, 1998).

Personal Security Inventory (PSI). This paper-and-pencil psychological test exists in various forms throughout the United States. For example, the California Personality Inventory (CPI), the Minnesota Multiphasic Personality Inventory (MMPI), and the Inwald Personality Inventory (IPI) are some of the more well known versions of the PSI. The advantages to these tests are they can be administered on company property and are relatively inexpensive. (Fischer and Green, 1998). These tests have the same problems as aptitude and skill-based test.

Psychological Stress Evaluator (PSE). While the PSI is a paper-and-pencil exam, the PSE is a machine that measurers changes in voice quality from tension in the vocal cords. Readouts from the PSE are recorded on a paper tape and responses analyzed by charting the reactions to various questions. This procedure allows a properly trained operator to establish an individual's response when lying (Fischer and Green, 1998).

The Polygraph or "Lie Detector". Polygraph tests are seldom admissible in criminal court. However, before 1997 these tests were used frequently by private employers. With the passage of the federal Employee Polygraph Protection Act of 1988, four types of employer behavior were prohibited. This act prohibits most private employers from requesting, requiring, suggesting, or causing job applicants or current employees to submit to a polygraph test as a condition of employment or as a condition of keeping their current job. Second, employers may not discharge, discipline, or make adverse employment decisions based on an employee's refusal to take the test. Third, employers are prohibited from using or asking about the results of a lie detector test given to either an employee or job applicant. Finally, employers may not retaliate against an applicant or employee for filing a complaint or otherwise asserting their rights under this federal law (Fischer and Green, 1998; Joel, 1996; Player, 1992; Wendover, 1995).

Note, however, that this law does not cover federal, state, or local government employees,

employees of the Department of Defense (DOD) or Federal Bureau of Investigation (FBI) contractors. In addition, employers for drug and pharmaceutical companies can require employees to take a polygraph if the applicants will have a job that allows direct access to controlled drugs. Finally, security companies have been granted an exception. This exception only applies to applicants for certain security positions. Applicants who will primarily be engaged in handling, trading, transferring, or storing "currency, negotiable instruments, proprietary information" can be required to take a polygraph.

This law does not allow the polygraphing of security alarm or guard services provided to other types of business or to private homes. Also non-security personnel within qualified companies are not required to take a lie detector test. Finally, companies that hire employees for their own company's security are not required to take such tests (Joel, 1996; Steingold, 1997).

Workplace theft or other misconduct which is costing the company money can lead an employer to request that employees take a lie detector test. However, the employer must meet four conditions. First, the test must be given in conjunction with an ongoing investigation of economic loss. Second, the employee must have had access to the missing property. Next, the employer must have reasonable suspicion that the employee was involved in the incident or activity. Last, the employer must give the employee a written notice of the incident being investigated and the reason the employee is considered a suspect at least 48 hours before the test (Joel, 1996; Player, 1992). Even if the employer meets the above guidelines, the employee cannot be disciplined or discharged solely on the basis of the results of the polygraph test or for refusing to take the exam (Fischer and Green, 1998).

What makes these honesty tests controversial centers on the issue of accuracy (Fischer and Green, 1998; Gorrill, 1974; Wendover, 1995). The American Management Association conducted a survey in 1990 that report only 6.2% of responding businesses used integrity tests in their screening process (Wendover, 1995). There are several reasons why employers do not use these exams. One reason is that these tests are often inaccurate. They may invade a person's right to privacy. Another reason may be the tests violate the ADA if an applicant must use any impaired skills, unless they are required for the job. Honesty tests may reflect test-taking ability rather than actual job skills which may discriminate against minority applicants (Steingold, 1997; Wendover, 1995).

Physical Examinations

Medical examinations in industry first started in the days when children were employed in the mines and cotton mills and labor was often obtained from workhouses. Today, there are three reasons why companies may require a pre-employment physical examination. First, to safeguard the health and safety of others. Second, to safeguard the health of vulnerable groups. The last reason for a physical exam is to safeguard the health of those who are working with or around toxic or hazardous material (Malcolm, 1970).

Currently, both the ADA and the Vocational Rehabilitation Act of 1973 impact on the employer's ability to request pre-employment medical examinations (Joel, 1996; Player, 1992). Under the ADA, pre-employment medical examinations and medical history questions are prohibited (Player, 1992; Steingold, 1997). However, during the pre-employment phase, employers may ask applicants limited questions concerning their ability to do specific, job-related tasks. One example would be asking a person who applied for a job loading trucks if he or she can lift 60 pounds. This type of question would be legal. But, an employer could not ask the applicant during the pre-employment phase if they had a "back" problem (Player, 1992).

Employers can make job offers conditional on passing a medical examination if two conditions are met. All medical results must be maintained in separate, confidential files and all employees in the job category are given the examination. Once these two conditions are met, employers can then ask questions that they could not ask during the pre-employment stage. Employers may ask questions about previous illnesses, diseases, or medications, and can request doctors to probe the applicant to make sure that the person can perform the job without posing a direct threat to their health or safety or that of others.

If a medical examination or inquiry results in the withdrawal of a conditional job offer, the employer must be able to show that:

- the reasons were job-related and consistent with business necessity, or
- The person was excluded to avoid a direct threat to health and safety, and
- no reasonable accommodation could be made, or
- such an accommodation would cause undue hardship (Player, 1992: Steingold, 1997).

Drug and Alcohol Testing

According to U. S. Department of Labor estimates, drug and alcohol use cost employers $75 to $100 billion annually in lost time, accidents, health care, and workers' compensation cost. Job accidents are directly related to drug or alcohol use 65% of the time. Health care benefits claims are 16 times higher for abusers than for nonabusers, and absentee rates are 3 times higher for abusers than for nonabusers. Substance abusers are 6 times more likely than their co-workers to file a workers' compensation claim, according to the U. S. Department of Health and Human Services (Bahls, 1998).

In response to the economic costs of drug and alcohol abuse, four-fifths of the major companies now test job applicants and employees for substance abuse. It is estimated that one-third of all job seekers will be tested for alcohol and drug use this year, compared with less than 10% a decade ago (Greenberg, 1996; Hartwell, Steele, and French, 1996; Sujak, Villanova, and Daly, 1995). The overall trend for positive tests is decreasing, from a high of 18.1% in 1987 to 1.9% in 1995. This decrease reflects changes in testing policies, increasing numbers of employers testing employees and job applicants rather than a decline in substance abuse (Bahls, 1998; Greenberg, 1996).

The ADA, the Rehabilitation Act of 1973, and the Drug Free Workplace Act of 1988 impact on drug and alcohol testing. In addition, government regulations also have guidelines that employers in certain industries must follow. Because of these laws and regulations, employers and employees have a legal right to insist on a drug-free workplace (Joel, 1996, Steingold, 1997; Wendover, 1995).

Under the Drug Free Workplace Act of 1988, employers must establish policies and procedures if they use drug and alcohol testing, but the legislation of 1988 **does not require** drug and alcohol testings (Joel, 1996). Since drug and alcohol testing is considered a medical test, the ADA also applies. The ADA forbids all medical testing unless a conditional offer of employment has been made. Once a conditional job offer has been made, the employer can then proceed with drug and alcohol testing (Steingold, 1997). Some applicants can use the Vocational Rehabilitation Act of 1973 to avoid the testing issue. If applicants use this law, they must be willing to admit that they have abused drugs or alcohol and then they could claim the disability. Finally, the National Labor Relations Board requires companies engaging in collective bargaining to negotiate drug and alcohol testing before the implementation of a program (Wendover, 1995).

The Department of Defense (DOD) requires all employees in sensitive jobs (public health or safety) or which involve national security to be tested for drugs and alcohol. DOD may also test all job applicants. The federal Department of Transportation (DOT) requires random drug testing of employees in safety-sensitive jobs in industries regulated by the agency. These regulations also allow DOT to do pre-employment screening. Employees having access to protected areas of nuclear plants or those involved with plant emergency response operations will be tested for drugs and alcohol according to the Nuclear Regulatory Commission regulations (Joel, 1996).

Remember, drug and alcohol testing is not required by federal law, but some federal agencies may regulate drug and alcohol testing requirements. Be careful to define why screening for drug and alcohol is important to your organization if federal regulations do not require it. Failure to follow appropriate rules may result in litigation. Remember there are numerous federal and state laws that protect employees from discrimination in the hiring process (Fletcher, 1997a; Flynn, 1996; Steingold, 1997; Sujak et al., 1995; Wendover, 1995).

AIDS Testing

In a 1987 U. S. Supreme Court decision three factors where listed that could be used to determine whether an employee could be fired or an applicant could be refused a job because of any contagious disease. To use this court decision, employers must examine the nature, duration and severity of the risk, the potential to harm others, and the probability of transmission. With AIDS the first two factors may be significant, but the third is virtually impossible to meet while at work (Joel, 1996).

Again, recall that the ADA prohibits medical testing until a job offer has been conditionally made. Persons with AIDS are listed as qualified disabled individuals under the ADA and this restricts medical testing to job related skills and conditions consistent with business necessities

(Joel, 1996; Player, 1992: Steingold, 1997).

INVESTIGATING JOB APPLICANTS

Prospective employers know the key to effective hiring rests on quality information about the job applicant. Poor hiring decisions are costly. For example, a business that operates on an 8% margin must add about $12,500 in gross revenue for every $1,000 lost to turnover costs (Arnesen, Fleenor, and Blizinsky, 1998).

Job Screening

Approximately 20% of all companies do not perform any type of background investigation (Arthur, 1997; Gips, 1998). Table 2 shows the percentage of companies that perform background investigations for each job category.

Table 2

Percentage of companies that perform background investigations for each job category.

Job Category	Percentage
Security Officer	72.8
Mid-level managers/supervisors	61.8
Security managers	60.7
Senior-level managers	49.7
Investigators	46.1
Other nonsupervisory full-time positions	43.5
Other nonsupervisory part-time positions	35.6
Maintenance/custodial crews	34.6
Top-level managers/CEOs	32.5
Consultants/contractors/vendors	24.1
Volunteers/interns	18.8
Other	18.8

Table 3 shows the most common types of employment records checks.

Table 3

Percentage of companies that perform the most common types of employment records checks.

Type of Employment Check	Percent of companies that perform the records check
Educational Records	81
Employment History Records	79
Reference Checks	59
Criminal Records	37
Motor Vehicle Records	21

(Arthur, 1997).

Figure 1 shows the percentage of applicants who were disqualified due to background screening. Most organizations disqualified fewer than 1 in 10 applicants due to background screening.

Percentage

25.8

11.2

21.2

5.9

2.9

16.5

6.5

10

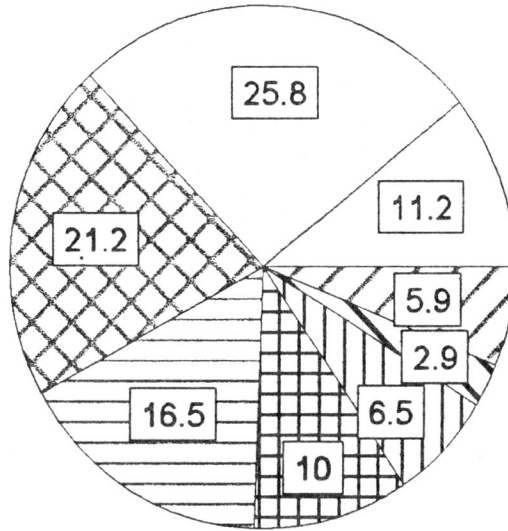

Number of Applicant's Disqualified

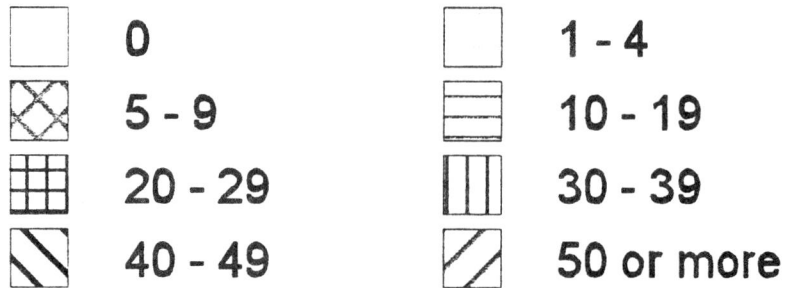

☐	0	☐	1 - 4
⊠	5 - 9	▤	10 - 19
⊞	20 - 29	⦀	30 - 39
▨	40 - 49	▨	50 or more

Figure 1: Percentage of applicants disqualified due to background investigations (Gips, 1998)

When organizations conducted background checks, 37% preferred to use internal resources, 30% used external resources, and the remaining 33% used a combination of the two methods (Gips, 1998).

Examining the Application

One of the first things an employer wants to do is have the applicant fill out a job application form. Application forms allow the company to determine what information it wants from the prospective employee, whereas the résumé allows the applicant to determine what information to volunteer. As stated previously, application forms should include a consent form as part of the application process. This form may be a separate form or could be part of the application form. The advantage of a separate document is that the employer can photocopy it and send it to people from whom the employer is seeking information (Steingold, 1997).

Next, an employer should look for obvious problems with the application form. For example, a person indicating that he or she went to school in New Mexico, lists no past residences located in New Mexico. Leaving blanks on the application form or answering with inappropriate responses are also "red" flags. For a security applicant an employer might ask if the person would use lawful force to carry out the job and the person answering states he only beats his wife, kids, and dog on Fridays. Employers need to take a sharp look at all dates provided on the application form. In the employment history, does the applicant list overlapping dates of employment for multiple jobs? It is possible that an applicant could be working two full time jobs for a short period of time, but, it would be more than unusual for an applicant to have worked three full time jobs. Also look for gaps in dates. Especially simultaneously gaps of 30, 60, and 90 days or 1, 5, or 10 years. These gaps may indicate that the person has been incarcerated.

Conducting External Checks

Now that the internal checking is done, the employer needs to verify external information. Remember, people will give false or incomplete information. By having the employee sign the consent form that was discussed above, employers reduce the risk of an invasion of privacy claim (Steingold, 1997).

References

Reference checks are used for two reasons. The first reason is to get some idea of whether an individual is suited to the job and how he or she will perform. Secondly, references are used to confirm the applicant is who they say they are and that they actually possess the experience and qualifications they claim to have (Fletcher, 1997b).

School Transcripts

On-the-job experience may be more important than a formal education. However, if education is part of the criteria for the job applicant then these records need to be verified (Steingold, 1997). When checking educational credentials, ask not only if the person attended the school, but the dates of attendance, the program or major studies, and whether he or she graduated (Wendover, 1995).

Credit Checks

It is permissible for an employer to conduct a credit check, especially if the potential employee will work with or have access to large sums of money. Credit checks are regulated by the Fair Credit Reporting Act (FCRA). The FCRA identifies employment as a "just reason" for an employer to check an potential employee's credit and it requires employers to disclose if the reason for not hiring was based on a credit check (Arthur, 1997; Robinson, 1997; Steingold, 1997; Wendover, 1995).

Criminal History Checks

For most private sector jobs, it is illegal to ask someone if they have been arrested, but inquiring about convictions is another matter. If applicants are rejected based on a criminal history check, the rejection should be based on some job-related function. Excluding everyone who has a prior criminal conviction could be a form of unlawful discrimination (Steingold, 1997).

Driving Records

If the job requires driving a vehicle, employers should check the driving records of all the applicants (Steingold, 1997). Employers may find that the person does not have a valid license or that it has been revoked by the state. Finally, employers need to discover if the applicant is a poor driver and has had numerous accidents or citations.

INTERVIEWING THE CANDIDATES

Interacting face-to-face with job candidates in an interview is the classic scenario for evaluating the employment hopefuls. Unfortunately, it also during this phase of the job search employers can make serious mistakes in questioning the applicants and in deciding who to hire. By understanding the subjective nature of interviewing, one can avoid selecting for apparent personality over abilities and experience. Most applicants are aware that the typical interview procedure will limit them to 15 minutes to an hour of one-on-one questioning by a member of management, and they will gear their preparation to that expectation. Anyone who is practiced can reflect an impressive or charming facade for that length of time, and even old hands at interviewing have fallen under the spell of an interviewee's charisma. To avoid this trap means focusing on the job and its description, and preparing a list of questions that will be asked of every job candidate without exception.

Write down a set of questions that zeroes in on the job duties and the applicant's skills. Be particularly careful to draw out experience in handling the same type or a related function the applicants have performed previously. By preparing a list and sticking to it throughout each interview, the risks are reduced that someone may complain about unequal treatment. Taking notes of each respondent's answers is valuable, too. This will allow for a comparison of the different candidates' responses without benefit of their personal delivery style. What may have sounded like a dynamite answer when delivered in person may on review be a real wet firecracker when compared to another applicant's flat but insightful and accurate analysis.

In addition to focusing on the relevant job skills being sought, it is critical for the interviewer to be alert for any answers that contradict what is documented on the applicant's resume. To be certain that this is not a simple matter of misinterpretation, ask for clarification, and carefully note down the answers. This is one acceptable digression from the structured, formal interview questions, providing an excellent opportunity to use *why* questions. Experienced interviewers are well aware that the *why* of what a person did is even more important than what the person actually did. In explaining the *why*, a person reveals his or her judgement, motivation, and personality.

Pay close attention to interviewees consistently failing to answer direct questions or those who are seemingly evasive in responding. Candidates that spend a lot of time complaining about their past employers, or concentrating on the job benefits and salary without displaying much interest in finding out about the job are obviously suspect. Even if their backgrounds are flawless, these may be warning signs of less than suitable employees.

Finally, do not ignore "gut" feelings about aspiring personnel. As a current employee of the company, no one is in a better position to know the people and situations existing in the workplace where the new employee will find him or herself. If all other qualifications of the candidates are equal, choosing the applicant that will complement the abilities of those already employed, or the one who will best fit into the workforce can be a matter of trusting one's instincts.

WORKING WITH THE NEW EMPLOYEE

Now that the search for an employee is over, it remains the responsibility of the hiring agency to orient the new worker to the job, the company environment, rules, and procedures. Whether this person is going to work in security or not, it is important that security personnel take part in the orientation process. Policies and their mandated procedures should be explained by those charged with their enforcement. Since security is often notified or involved in specific employee problems, they should be on hand to explain what actions should be reported, and to whom.

One such problem of growing concern is that of violence in the workplace. No longer a rarity, reports reflect that some type of violence has occurred in nearly one-third of all companies within the last five years. Even more alarming is the fact that an average of 15 people a week are murdered at their place of employment (Baron, 1993; Brandman, 1997).

Hoping that the multiple stages of personnel screening filtered out the worst of potentially dangerous people is understandable, but assuming that the process is 100% effective is foolhardy. High risk individuals do manage to slip through even the most rigorous of pre-hiring processes, and even long term, usually stable employees can be adversely effected by situational factors. Efforts to prevent such violence are not only necessary, but practical since relatively few violent acts in the workplace are spontaneous. Training employees to recognize warning signs, and requiring them to report all incidents without exception is the first step toward circumventing this problem.

Examples of actions that employees must report:

- All employees making threats or being threatened. Threats of any type should never be treated casually. Penalties for those failing to report these interactions should make it clear that all threats will be treated seriously.
- Employees who are suddenly terminated, or who are anticipating a layoff. Loss of livelihood can trigger anxiety and rage.
- Employees using alcohol or drugs. Any substances that lower inhibitions or are mood-altering can cause employees to act out of character.
- Employees with serious problems at home. Domestic problems can easily spill over into the workplace. Such workplace confrontations can run the gamut from simple assault to homicide.

A security staff not educated in or alerted to these possible precursors of violence cannot execute the necessary steps to intervene or prevent the aggression. Whether the solution involves tightening physical security to bar outside visitors or former personnel, or referring the worker to the company's employee assistance program, the security department will need notification of the problem to act. Company policies, education programs, and enforcement helps insure all levels of employees become aware that they must contribute to diverting violence from the workplace.

There are a number of other Human Resource problems that require the knowledge and attention of security personnel. Some of these may be related to, or exacerbate the previously discussed unstable or potentially violent individual. For example, a high absenteeism rate and consistent tardiness can actually be symptoms of a larger problem. Reasons for both behaviors can include the misuse of alcohol, drugs (licit and illicit), and depression. Similarly, a high rate of attrition can be a clear indicator of in-house morale problems. The cost of attracting, hiring, and training qualified personnel makes losing them an expensive proposition. If a person's individual problems or a supervisor's management style is costing the employer valuable human resources, the issue should be recognized and dealt with. Non-malicious, objective assessment of these types of employee problems often falls within the purview of security.

An additional Human Resource problem that may involve company security is the investigation of sexual harassment complaints. A general definition of sexual harassment would be any unwanted attention from anyone in the workforce that is sexual in nature and may result in job interference or discomfort to the individual (Myers, D., 1984). Sources of sexual harassment range from supervisors to employee co-workers, and can even be caused by non-workers having contact with the employee in the workplace. Regardless of who engages in the activity, the courts are holding employers liable for everything from the acts of both employees and non-employees as well as acts for which the management may not be aware. Companies are also being held accountable for prevention and awareness programs, and are expected to take prompt corrective action when sexual harassment is discovered.

Clearly, companies need to develop and implement strategies that outline preventative and corrective measures for the problem. A "no tolerance" stance by the company proscribing unequivocally that sexual harassment will not be tolerated and any person found to be in violation of the policy statement will be subject to discipline, even termination is a standard beginning to dealing with the issue. Once this is established, a grievance procedure must be designed that allows complainants to make their complaints known. This may include reporting the problem to security, especially in any cases where the complainant's manager is the alleged perpetrator of the offense. Investigations and hearing in these matters need to be conducted in a fair and impartial way, and such complaints must be handled with dispatch. Delay in these matters creates more suspicion and ill-will on the part of the reporting person. Additionally, if the grievance is sustained and harassment in fact occurred, a decision must be promptly made and corrective action immediately implemented.

FIRING EMPLOYEES

Probably one of the most uncomfortable acts anyone in a supervisory position must perform is firing an employee. While there are a lot of oblique ways to "encourage" a problematic employee to resign, most such actions fall along a continuum ranging from unethical to outright illegal behavior. The best method for terminating someone's employment is still the direct approach.

The first step in a termination decision is determining exactly why the person is being fired. The reason for severing the individual should be concrete and verifiable. In most cases, the company will have established a set of procedures that must be followed and documented prior to actual termination. Usually this progresses from a talk with the employee about the problem, then a written warning, and finally the official firing.

When all other avenues have been explored without success, the time has come to end the employment of a worker. Confronting the issue instead of delaying, deferring or avoiding it will be easier if certain suggestions and strategies are followed.

- **Do not prolong termination.** It is not a good idea to keep the employee on the payroll until he or she relocates. The person's interests and energy will be directed toward a new job search, and the damage he or she may inflict on the company in terms of physical destruction, theft, sabotage or morale are incalculable. Despite the initial shock of termination, such action is better for employee and agency alike.

- **Arrange to tell the employee at the end of the day and week.** Telling someone he or she is fired and leaving the person to continue working as if nothing has happened is an act of cruelty. It is also a dangerous act, as the newly fired employee may be resentful enough to cause trouble.
- **Be direct, clear, and honest.** Tell the person directly that they are being fired and exactly why. Be blunt, but not brutal, maintaining eye contact throughout the notification. Avoid the use of euphemisms like "we're letting you go" or "we can't use you anymore." Fuzzy language may seem more humane, but can actually foster false hopes.
- **Do not apologize or give hope.** Once the message of "you're fired" has been delivered, resist the very real temptation of softening the blow by saying "I'm sorry." Express concern and personal regret in nonverbal ways, and allow the employee a chance to blow off steam without interruption. Do not make patronizing statements as "someday you'll see this really was all for the best." Do not communicate anything to the person being fired that in any way makes the firing decision seem tentative or subject to appeal. Make it clear that this is a **final** decision.
- **Make a record of all that has been said.** This record should cover both sides of the conversation. Make a careful note of any threats, innuendoes, and/or accusations.
- **Inform the other employees.** Announce the firing decision to the other employees as soon as possible after informing the person being terminated . Make this announcement only when the employee is not present. Informing the co-workers quickly acts to cut down on speculation and rumors that an emotional issue like firing generates. Announce the act directly. "Pete has been fired." Then respond to questions carefully, keeping in mind that charges of libel are a real possibility if too much is said (Preston, P., 1982).

Immediately restrict the reasons for the fired employee to be on premises. If that person has too many personal items on company grounds to remove at one time, arrange an appointment for him or her to return, informing them that security personnel will escort that individual during retrieval of the property. Once an individual has been fired, it is imperative that all security personnel be made aware that the person has been terminated, and what dismissal means to his or her rights of access to different areas within the company complex.

CONCLUSION

As this chapter illustrates, hiring, retaining, and firing is risky but essential business. Security and management must work together to keep up with federal employment legislation and commit to assigning resources to attract and verify the quality of applicants. They must also agree to policies, procedures, and enforcement that will keep the workplace safe.

Admittedly, no systems or guidelines will insure a workplace free of conflict or litigation. The unpredictability of human beings guarantees surprises. But a dedicated attempt to hire and retain the best employees possible will lower the risks to an acceptable level.

References

Arthur, A. 1997. "How much should employers know?" *Black Enterprise*, 28, 56.

Arnesen, D. W., Fleenor, C. P., & Blizinsky, M 1998. "Name, rank, and serial number? The dilemma of reference checks." *Businesses Horizons*, 41, 19-38.

Bahls, J. E. 1998. "Drugs in the workplace." *HR Magazine*, 43, 80-87.

Baron, S. A. 1993. *Violence in the workplace; A prevention and management guide for businesses.* Ventura, CA: Pathfinder Publishing of California.

Brandman, B. 1997. "Fight workplace violence." *Transportation and Distribution*, 38, p 87-88.

Dobrish, C., Wolff, R., & Zevnik, B. 1984. *Hiring the right person for the right job.* New York: Franklin Watts.

Doele, D.C. & Dukes, C. W. 1986. "Skills inventories and promotion systems." In J. J. Famularo (Ed.) *Handbook of human resource administration* (2nd ed; pp 18-1 - 18-21). New York: McGraw-Hill Book Co.

Fischer, R. J. & Green, G. 1998. *Introduction to security* (6th ed). Boston: Butterworth-Heinemann.

Fletcher, C. 1997b. "Not all candidates are who they say they are." *Peoples Management,* 3, 51.

Fletcher, M. 1997a. "Making pre-employment screening work." *Business Insurances,* 31, 91.

Flynn, G. 1996. "Will drug testing pass or fail in court?" *Personnel Journal,* 75, 141.

Gorrill, B. E. 1974. *How to prevent losses and improve profits with effective personnel security procedures.* Homewood, IL: Dow Jones-Irwin, Inc.

Greenberg, E. R. 1996. "Drug-testing now standard practice." *HR Focus*, 73, 24.

Gips, M. 1998, November. "Screen test." *Security Management*, p.13.

Hartwell, T. D., Steele, P. D., & French, M. T. 1996. "Prevalence of drug testing in the workplace." *Monthly Labor Review*, 119, 35-42.

Jessup, G. 1970. "Testing trade skills." In B. Ungerson (Ed.) *Recruitment handbook* (pp. 140-152). London: Gower Press.

Joel III, L. G. 1996. *Every employee's guide to the law: Everything you need to know about your rights in the workplace–and what to do if they are violated.* New York: Pantheon.

Mali, M. 1986. "Testing and the employment procedure." In J. J. Famularo (Ed.) *Handbook of human resource administration* (2nd ed; pp 15-1 - 15.20). New York: McGraw-Hill Book Co.

Malcolm, D. 1970. "Physical Testing." In B. Ungerson (Ed.) *Recruitment handbook* (pp 94-106). London: Gower Press.

Myers, D. W. 1984. *Establishing and building employee assistance programs.* London: Quorum Books.

Player, M. A. 1992. *Federal law of employment discrimination in a nutshell* (3rd ed). St. Paul, MN: West.

Preston, P. 1982. *Employer's guide to hiring and firing.* Englewood Cliffs: Prentice-Hall.

Robinson, E. A. 1997. "Beware–job seekers have no secrets." *Fortune,* 136, 285.

Siegel, P. J. & Bryant, M. R. 1997. "A hiring checklist." *HR Focus,* 74, 22.

Steingold, F. S. 1997. *The employer's legal handbook* (2nd ed). Berkeley, CA: Nolo Press.

Sujak, D. A., Villanova, P., & Daly, J. P. 1995. "The effects of drug-testing program characteristics on applicants' attitudes toward potential employment." *The Journal of Psychology,* 129, 401-416.

Wendover, R. W. 1995. *Smart hiring.* Naperville, IL: Small Business Sourcebooks.

CHAPTER 8

TECHNOLOGY: UNLOCKING THE FUTURE FOR SECURITY PRACTITIONERS

Steven R. Keller, CPP
Principal Consultant
Steven R. Keller and Associates, Inc.

The importance of knowledge in the areas of access control, key control, CCTV, computers, alarm systems, locks, and fire systems is explained. A well rounded loss prevention person must have at least a cursory knowledge in all areas.

For many years, the security officer was a mere watchman, or a potted palm, stationed in a lobby to watch without authority to act, the comings and goings of all. His boss was a building superintendent or perhaps another guard or a bureaucrat who lacked much understanding of security as a profession. Under the best (or worst) conditions, security personnel had only to be "toughs," physically better than those they "policed." Those with brains need not apply for the position, and the most complicated piece of equipment the security practitioner had to operate was a door lock.

Within the past twenty-five years, a new generation of security manager has developed, and organizations such as The American Society for Industrial Security have been born which advocate higher standards and certifications. In the early days, the security manager was still a second class citizen within his organization, and he lacked any real role in the general management of the firm.

I am a super-achiever. After an active five years on the Washington, D.C. police force, I joined a federal government agency as a Special Agent. Soon I was placed in the position of Assistant Director of Security for the entire agency. I recall discussing career options with a friend in the Personnel Department. I was told not bother to applying for openings outside the security operation since security personnel were "earmarked" as being unacceptable for general management positions regardless of talent or success.

That same year, I spent $145 -- a pretty good sum for someone who took home $175 per week -- for my first electronic calculator. It was small, but twice the size of a typical calculator most of us own today. I don't know why I needed it but I knew that I had to have one. Even my department budget was done for me by a bureaucrat who knew more about my operation than I did -- at least in the eyes of my superiors.

Those two events -- the revelation that I was on a dead-end career path and the purchase of one of the first pocket calculators, were related. During the next year, my agency lost hundreds of small calculators off of desks, their small size making them vulnerable to the cleaning crews and the deliverymen who steal from offices daily as they move through the Washington, D.C. labyrinth of buildings. But it really didn't matter. Within months, the calculators were outdated, replaced by increasingly less expensive models until a typical credit card size calculator -- small enough that it rarely sat vulnerable on a desk -replaced all of the high priced, less powerful models that remained.

The year the calculator began to shrink marked the beginning of a revolution. The technological revolution, that is. It was a whole new ballgame! And along with the explosion of technology came the explosion in security technology. I no longer wanted to leave the exciting field of security electronics and technology. I wanted to grow with it. The growth potential was, and still is, unlimited.

I look back at my peers -- men and women who had left the police department in the mid 1970's -- to pursue security careers. Some made the "big time" solely on their management expertise. But most were displaced by a whole new generation of security practitioner who knew his way around a computer and had a sound basic understanding of other aspects of technology. Today, when I look at those who are "making the big bucks," I see that most have, at least, kept up with basic security technology. But what I see beyond the current generation of security manager is a generation that has mastered at least some advanced areas of security technology and have a sound basis of understanding of many others.

So what does it take to be a success in the new era of security? While there is still an emphasis on management, a well rounded security practitioner will have to keep ahead of the technological revolution and its security applications. Security managers are increasingly becoming part of the overall corporate management team. They are expected to know about the business of the business they serve. That means that if you want to be Director of Corporate Security for an airline, you had better learn about how airlines operate. In any case, you better know how to read a corporate annual report. Probably most important in the management area is the need to be articulate, orally and in writing. If I were hiring a security manager today, I'd want him -- or her -- to be a business person who had made a successful transition into security and then moved up the ranks gaining practical experience in management and security technology.

What technical skills are needed? Unless you earn an electrical engineering degree in college, they really don't teach many security technology courses! First of all, if you don't know how to operate a personal computer the day you enter the security field, you don't have a prayer in a security career in coming years. Students interested in entering just about any career today had better master one of the major integrated software packages which include a word processor, data base, spread sheet, and modem communications package. And you better know personal computer hardware, too. If you don't have a basic understanding of what a computer is and how it works, you're in big trouble before you begin.

Why is this so critical? Not only is the modern security manager expected to manage, he is expected to do spread sheet analysis of budgets, loss projections, pay raise analysis, etc. He must prepare memorandums requiring more than basic word processing skills and he must master, completely, a variety of data base skills to enable him to use the power of a computer to his advantage as a manager. Gone are the days when incident reports can efficiently be kept on paper or scheduling done on an old fashioned legal pad. Investigative files occupy a data base and even disaster plans and call-up lists are computerized.

Of course, the personal computer is becoming an important component in the alarm and access control systems in use today. The best way to be regarded by your boss as the "Lead Guard" or to be earmarked as inadequate for company management is to fail to learn to use the power of a computer.

The security practitioner of the present and future must know the latest in security equipment. Subscriptions to the major security magazines and journals is critical. Many old time practitioners make the mistake of reading only materials that interest them. The successful practitioner will read everything he can get his hands on including -- and especially -- the ads! On a daily basis, the successful security manager will read the *New York Times* and the *Wall Street Journal* and on a monthly basis, he will read *Security Management, Security,* and as many of the other more specialized security publications as he can, such as CCTV and Access Controls. If there are security newsletters in your field of specialty, subscribe to them. "Hotel/Motel Security and Safety Management" and their counterpart newsletters for college and hospital administrators often have in depth discussions of technical and non-technical matters. And the general management "trades" as they are called, the monthly magazines directed toward non-security managers in your field, such as *Museum News, The Journal of Property Management* or *Shopping Centers Today* are essential reading.

I am a collector of, what are called in the security and building industry, "catalog cut sheets." Catalog cuts are advertisements for various products such as components of security systems such as motion detectors, alarm panels, locks, etc. that also contain operational data and specifications. There is hardly a security product available or that has been available in the past 10 years, that is not on file in my office in the form of a cut sheet. I am also an avid user of "reader reply cards" found in most security journals. I attend security trade shows as often as I can, specifically to gather information on security products and equipment. If I don't understand a particular product after the cut sheet, I ask someone who can explain it to me.

I've received most of my technical security knowledge by asking the right questions of the right people. When I attend security trade shows, I try to catch the most important seminar programs. However, unlike many of my colleagues, I save time for a thorough review of the exhibits. In fact, I often spend days in the exhibits. While most attendees are in seminars, I'm spending time with the representatives who are selling a product about which I want -- or need -- to know. I plan my time in the exhibits when I don't have to compete with too many others. It gives me the opportunity for personal interaction and questions.

When I approach an exhibit booth, I ask "Who's the salesman here?" That's the guy I don't want to talk to. And I don't want to talk to the pretty model hired to spew out a canned sales pitch about the product. When I've identified the salesman, I seek out the technician and let him explain to me what the product is, and how it works. Now that's how you learn something!

There are several major areas of security technology that are especially important to know. They are:

1.   Large security systems.
These systems are computer-based, meet high security "standards" as defined by Underwriters Laboratories (UL) or the Department of Defense (DOD), and often integrate burglar alarm, fire alarm, access control, CCTV, and related systems. They are designed for large installations or very high security situations.

2.   Small alarm systems.
These are generally referred to as "alarm panels" but also include affiliated control equipment such as digital communicators that transmit an alarm signal to a monitoring site. The variety of alarm panels is great, and the security practitioner must know the correct application for each type of panel.

3.   Interior and exterior alarm initiating and alarm indicating devices.
Initiating devices are detectors, from switches to motion and sound detectors, that catch the crook. Alarm indicating devices report the catch to the alarm panel or computer by doing something. Simple alarm indicating devices are bells or horns, and more sophisticated indicating devices are limited only by the imagination. The various alarm components are the basis of most security systems and understanding the various technologies of detection such as infrared, microwave, ultrasonic, sound discrimination, and verified technology, to name a few, is absolutely essential. One must know how each technology works, the causes of false alarms for each technology, and the best way of applying specific detectors and alarm indicators in specific situations.

4.   Fire Systems.
Know everything you can learn about fire systems. As the role of the security professional expands, it expands into the area of fire protection, safety and risk management. Fire systems, like security systems, use alarm initiating devices and alarm indicating devices and you must know the best application for each. Not unimportant is the need to know about fire suppression systems. While it is not as important for the security professionals to have the depth of knowledge regarding sprinklers, extinguishers and similar suppression technologies, a basic working knowledge is useful. Increasingly, we have become "protection" professionals, not just "security" professionals.

5.   CCTV Systems.
Closed circuit television cameras, monitors, mounts, recorders, enclosures, lenses, and related equipment are important knowledge for us all, as CCTV is playing an important role in modern

security. Learn about the means used to transmit TV images first as fiber optics, microwave, and various hard wired technologies. And learn about digital transmission of TV signals. Slow scan television and transmission of CCTV signals over phone lines, by radio signal, and over alarm wires is the trend of the future.

6. Locks.
Know about locks, both mechanical and electronic. Know about access control systems including electronic door strikes and magnetic release locks. Know about card key technology and biometrics. Know about key control and key control equipment. A full understanding of the electronic access control technology is a must in most corporate environments.

7.   Security Communications.
Know how alarm signals are transmitted. Know the technology involved and the equipment required. Know how alarm signals are defeated in transmission.

8.   Security Containers.
It is important to know about cash boxes, key boxes, safes, and vaults. Know about weapons cabinets, document destruction systems, and document waste disposal products. In security, there are a vast number of instances where you must protect valuables by containerizing them. You cannot perform this responsibility if you do not know the vast market on security containers.

9.   Fences, glazing, hardware and barriers.
Learn about bullet resistant glass, hollow metal door products, and fence protection systems. Know what the market holds today and where it seems to be going in the future.

10.   Understand security electronic systems.
Battery back-up units, generators, power supplies, and transformers.

Of course, there are other areas that are important as well. But the above will get you started. Learn as much about these technologies and the related equipment as you can by introducing yourself to the products in catalogs, in journals, and on display in trade shows.

But to know about security hardware and technology is not enough. It is important to know security standards as well. Read everything you can about Underwriters Laboratories, Factory Mutual, and similar technology standards. Ascertain what standards apply to a specific technology and learn what the standard requires. You can get this information by discussing standards with the manufacturer of a product, then reading the standard itself, available from the standard setting organization.

Learn about the National Fire Protection Association and their National Fire Codes. And fully understand the Life Safety Code, also distributed by the NFPA. Many of the logical security countermeasures against crime in a facility are not available to us due to fire code restrictions that facilitate quick egress in an emergency. There are other codes and standards, as well, that affect security. Standards for lighting, for example, are critical. And then there are the *de facto* standards. A number of legal case law newsletters are available which outline current trends in security litigation and serve as *de facto* standards on how much security is legally enough in a particular environment. Light levels, alarm requirements, etc. are all affected by court cases.

The modern security professional must understand how security can be designed into a building during its initial construction, or retrofitted during renovation. Therefore, a basic understanding of construction techniques, the construction process, and certain important construction related skills are necessary. Every modern security manager, for example, must be able to read blueprints and specifications, and should have a good sound grasp of how they apply to the corporate security program: know and understand the steps in the construction process and have a thorough understanding of your company's procurement requirements, during construction and under day to day operating conditions.

Probably most important of all is the ability to adapt technology to your specific situation. Say, for example, that you become Director of Security for a major art museum, responsible for the protection of a million dollars in irreplaceable art. Not only must you keep more assets on hand than any bank in your city, but you also must hang these assets on the walls for all to see and approach, rather than store them safely in a vault. You must protect your collection, handicapped by a set of "rules" that apply to work in museums. These rules, among other things, say that security cannot be too visible, detectors must not be too obtrusive, you may not touch the pictures in any way with sensors or wires, you may not place anything in front of the picture such as glass or protective glazing as this will interfere with the ability to see the fine brush strokes. But you find that few companies make a product specifically designed to help you overcome the limitations placed on you in the field of museum security. So you have to improvise. With your knowledge and skills in the area of security technology, you adapt equipment made for one task to the unique task required of you. That's what sets you apart from others. That is what makes you an asset to your employer.

Your ability to excel in a technologically changing world will depend upon your ability to keep pace with the security technology. Know the trends. Know how new technology is being applied to solve current problems. Your ability to foresee the changes in technology will enable you to make wise business decisions for your employer. Why buy old technology when you can buy technology that is on the leading edge? But how will you know, if you don't keep pace?

Learn how to identify trends. CCTV cameras get smaller and computers get smarter. It seems like only yesterday that we were all impressed that alarms no longer had to be annunciated by a blinking light but instead printed out on a 'teletype" printer. Then everyone began to build proprietary, private label central processors to analyze alarm data and display it on a computer monitor. But these were expensive and out of reach for many of us. I remember telling everyone to buy computer-based systems that utilized IBM PC's to process incoming data. Why buy a proprietary computer that could only be repaired by one vendor when you could buy a computer that could be repaired at any local computer store? People thought I was crazy! I remember telling a product manufacturer how nice it would be to have a watch patrol system that used a hand held reader to scan universal product code stickers. Presto! Now they are old hat! Then came color graphics on alarm systems, touch command screens, and cameras so small they can be concealed just about anywhere. Today, cellular phone technology offers alternate alarm signal transmission means, but I'm sure that by tomorrow, we'll be sending signals directly to the central station via the satellite using a more 'modern" means. When the technology is ready, I will be ready to use it. If you plan to get to the top, you will have to be ready too.

Prepare for your career in security by studying basic electronics and computer technology. You don't have to be a computer programmer to be successful. Your needs will require that you understand computers and know how to adapt existing applications programs. A basic course in mechanical engineering won't hurt, either. But concentrate your formal education in the areas of business management, unless your school offers a specific curriculum in alarm system or similar technologies. Learn how to read a company balance sheet and annual report. Know how to do a budget. And above all -- read my lips -- know how to write a good memo and lead a meeting in an articulate and professional manner. Without these skills, you'll be the potted plant, the "Lead Guard," whose security department is run by others!

The security industry offers a variety of highly specialized courses but you have to be on a mailing list to learn of them. Members of the American Society for Industrial Security and readers of major security trade publications regularly get mailings about technical courses, and courses are offered at the International Security conferences and the American Society for Industrial Security annual meetings, both held annually. And the premiere security technical journal "ST&D", standing for *Security Technology and Design* (http://www.simon-net.com) brings monthly information that is not to be missed by any security professional.

Finally, the security professional and the student of security management can fall back on the time tested, "internship." Too few internships are offered today because employees and students expect to be compensated for their time as though they had technical skills to offer. If more students understand that an internship offers them an education that money cannot buy, they would jump at any opportunity to work for a locksmith, alarm installer, or learning the ropes as an intern in a modern security department office in an industry they have targeted for their career. There is no better training than "doing!" If I had to learn technical security today, I'd do it differently. Rather than working my way through college in a factory earning minimum wage, I'd volunteer, if necessary, to spend my summers working with a locksmith, an alarm installer, and a successful security consultant.

Too many security managers and students of the profession never learn that it is not up to their teacher to teach them but it is up to them to learn from their teachers. The best way to learn about security technology is to read everything that is written and ask how it applies to their specific field. Grasp the basic concept of how security technology works, and everything else falls into place.

CHAPTER 9

COMPUTER SECURITY: THE NEW NECESSITY

Kenneth A. Clontz, Ph.D.
Department of Law Enforcement
and Justice Administration
Western Illinois University

Computer technology is transforming the way America works and plays. People across the country are utilizing the computers' speed and data managing power to solve a myriad of social, financial, and educational problems. It is not a slow, evolutionary process in which law, ethics, public and private organizations can comfortably adjust. It is a sudden explosion and all pervasive rush into an uncharted region of applications and innovations. High-tech terms such as information brokers, cashless society, paperless culture, and electronic pathways have been coined by social scientists in an attempt to understand and explain this transformation (Magel, 1991).

TYPES OF COMPUTER SYSTEMS

Four general categories of computer systems are available today: microcomputers, minicomputers, mainframe computers, and super computers. What separates these categories from one another is how much information the computer can store, the processing speed of the system, and the size of the computer system (Sawyer, Williams, and Hutchinson, 1995; Slotnick et al., 1986). Microcomputers will begin this discussion.

Microcomputers

These are the smallest and cheapest of the four categories. Microcomputers are designed primarily for individuals or small businesses. Therefore, these systems can fit either on or beside a person's desktop (Covington, 1991; Rothman and Mosmann, 1985; Slotnick et al., 1986). Within this category are two types of computers: personal computers (PCS) and workstations (Sawyer et al., 1995).

Personal Computers (PCS)

These machines can sit on a desk, stand on the floor, or are portable, and are either IBM or Apple compatible. Both systems can operate easy-to-use programs such as word processing, spreadsheets, and data management (Covington, 1991; Sawyer et al., 1995; Slotnick et al., 1986).

Nonportable PCS require an AC outlet and weigh more than 20 pounds. These systems do not require special installation requirements (i.e., extra air conditioning, heavy duty wiring, etc.). With desktop and floor-standing computers, the user can add circuit boards to the system. For example, these boards can include modems, scanners, video capture systems, and fax machines. The following are nonportable PCS:

Desktops are machines that can fit on a single table or desk. A difficulty with this system is how much space the cabinet "footprint" occupies (Sawyer et al., 1995; Slotnick et al., 1986).

Floor-Standing computers are those in which the system cabinet sits as a "tower" on the floor next to the desk (Sawyer et al., 1995).

Luggable systems weigh between 20 and 25 pounds. These systems contain all the components (monitor, computer, and keyboard) in one unit. Sometimes they include a printer. These machines are also called transportable because they are designed to be moved but not to be used in transit (Covington, 1991; Sawyer et al., 1995; Slotnick et al., 1986).

Portable computers do not require an AC outlet. Instead these machines operate from a battery. Weight for portables range from 1/2pound to 20 pounds. Portable systems are designed to be used in transit. These systems do not have special installation requirements (i.e., extra air conditioning, heavy duty wiring, etc.). The following are portable PCS:

Laptop computers weigh between 8 - 20 pounds. These systems have a flat display screen, which can display mono or color images. In 1991, some retail stores claimed that one out of every three new computers they sold were laptops (Covington, 1991; Sawyer et al., 1995).

Notebook computers get their name from their size, which is roughly the size of a thick notebook and weighs between four and 7.5 pounds. These machines can easily be tucked into a briefcase, backpack, or simply under your arm (Covington, 1991 -, Sawyer et al., 1995).

Sub-notebooks weigh between 2.5 and 4 pounds.

Pocket PCS weigh about 1 pound. These computers are also called handhelds and are useful in specific situations. Pocket PCS may be classified as either electronic organizers, palmtop computers, or personal digital assistants (PDAS) or personal communicators (Sawyer et al., 1995).

Pen computers are often the size of a sub-notebook or pocket computer. These machines lack a keyboard or mouse but allow the user to enter data by writing directly on the screen with a stylus or pen (Sawyer et al., 1995).

Workstations

Workstations look like desktop PCS but are more powerful. These systems cost between $10,000 and $150,000 (Sawyer et al., 1995).

Minicomputers

Minicomputers make up the middle class of computer size and power. They are popular with small to medium-sized businesses because they can be used as a "server" and do not require special installation. "Servers" are central computers that hold data and programs for many PCS or terminals, called clients. These clients are linked by a computer network. The entire network is called a client-server network (Covington, 1991; Rothman and Mosmann, 1985; Sawyer et al., 1995; Slotnick et al., 1986).

Mainframes

Mainframe systems occupy specially wired, air-conditioned rooms and are the oldest category of computers. Mainframe computers are capable of great processing speed and data storage allowing multiple users to utilize this system simultaneously. Because of their costs (between $50,000 and $5 million) large organizations use these systems, with a staff of professional programmers and technicians (Covington, 1991; Rothman and Mosmann, 1985; Sawyer et al., 1995; Slotnick et al., 1986),

Supercomputers

The largest and most powerful category of computers are called supercomputers. Such computers are high-capacity machines that also require special air-conditioned rooms, specially trained staff, and are the fastest calculating devices ever invented. To achieve this capability, cost (typically from $225,000 to more than $30 million) is set aside to achieve the maximum capabilities technology has to offer. Because of the cost, these machines are used primarily by government, large companies, and universities (Covington, 1991; Sawyer et al., 1995; Slotnick et al., 1986).

COMPUTER DATABASES

Computers have been fundamental in the development of "electronic data processing" departments across the country. For these information brokers, electronically organized facts have become their tools and products. The U.S. Labor Department estimates that by the year 2000, 80% of American workers will use computers and computer data on their jobs. Twenty years ago such a statistic was irrelevant, few computers existed except in the largest government and corporate agencies (Magel, 1991).

Keep in mind that a "database" is any organized collection of facts. Databases may serve many purposes or only one (Rothman and Mosmann, 1985; Slotnick et al., 1986). Databases are of three general types: personal, governmental, and business (Sawyer et al., 1995).

Personal Databases

One person normally uses this type of database and stores his or her information on some type of personal computer (Sawyer et al., 1995).

Government Databases

Within the U.S. Federal Government today, collecting, processing, and storing information on computers accounts for much of its quantifiable work. Government files fall into two broad categories: Law Enforcement and Social Service records (Rothman and Mosmann, 1985).

Law Enforcement

Since 1924, the Federal Bureau of Investigation (FBI) has been responsible for keeping the Nation's fingerprint and criminal history records. In 1967, National Crime Information Center (NCIC) was established. Today NCIC connects some 80,000 police agencies across the country through a telecommunications computer network to the FBI records division. More than 8 million records are stored in its computers, along with 213,000,000 civil and criminal fingerprints records. On a daily basis, the FBI receives more than 100,000 electronic requests for criminal history information, over 40,000 requests to search its fingerprint files, and 14,000 updates to its criminal history records (FBI Criminal Justice Information Services Division [FBI CJIS], 1996). Thousands of law enforcement personnel, both federal and state, depend on this information to perform their jobs.

Because of the vast amount of data being received and sent by the FBI, computer control of large volumes of data had to be developed. Without such control the data flow would be unmanageable. To meet this need the FBI developed the Criminal Justice Information Services (CJIS) Division located in West Virginia. This division, created in February 1992, consolidates the FBI's criminal justice information systems. CJIS initiatives include replacing the current National Crime Information Center (NCIC) system with the NCIC 2000 system, enhancing the current Uniform Crime Reporting (UCR) program through the implementation of the National Incident-Based Reporting System (NIBRS), and operating the Integrated Automated Fingerprint Identification System (IAFIS) (FBI CJIS, 1996)

The NCIC 2000 system augments existing NCIC functions. NCIC 2000 will provide increased capacity, updated technology, and additional fingerprint and image processing functions (Mackall, 1996a). New and improved capabilities associated with NCIC 2000 include:

- Image processing (i.e., mug shot, signature, and other identifying specialized and generic images) (Mackall, 1996a and 1996b).

- IAFIS. IAFIS will support a law enforcement agency's ability to digitally record individuals' fingerprints and other related information, and electronically exchange data with the FBI. When fully operational, IAFIS will completely replace the current paper-based system. This system will scan paper-based fingerprint cards, store fingerprint data digitally, automatically search the database to identify suspects, and dramatically reduce the number of manual steps needed to make a positive fingerprint identification. The entire IAFIS process will take on average 24 hours, with emergency requests being handled in as little as two hours (IAFIS: the Real Story, 1996).

- Access to new databases (e.g., Convicted Person on Supervised Release and Protection Order File). A Convicted Person on Supervised Release file will contain records of subjects under supervised release (probation or parole). Protection Order files maintain records of individuals who have been ordered to desist from violent or threatening acts or harassment against, or contact or communication with, or physical proximity to, another person. These files will also include temporary orders issued by civil or criminal courts. Implementation of this file is set for 1997 (Mackall, 1996a and 1996b).

- Linkage fields. These provide the ability to associate multiple records with the same criminal or the same crime (Mackall, 1996a).

- Access to five external databases (e.g., Interstate Identification Index (111), Canadian Police Information Center (CPIC), Federal Bureau of Prisons (Sentry), National Law enforcement Telecommunications system (NLETS), and the UCR National Incident Based Reporting System (NIBRS) (Mackall, 1996b).

Social Services

The Internal Revenue Service (IRS) is the federal government's largest computer user, processing over 95 million tax returns annually (Magel, 1991; Slotnick et al., 1986). Each is sorted by high speed bar-codes readers, checked for mathematical consistency and stored on magnetic tape. Later they are cross-checked and analyzed against information received from employers on supporting documents. IRS computers can process over 30,000 returns per hour. They also randomly select another 3,000 returns for an audit. Future IRS plans call for professional tax preparers to electronically submit tax returns by modem and telephone line. Refunds may be credited directly to tax payers' bank accounts. Under such a plan, acknowledgment of the receipt of the tax information could be made in a day and refunds issued within three weeks.

Other agencies in the Federal government likewise work with huge stores of information. It has been estimated that there are over 4 trillion dossiers on citizens in various government computer archives. This is an average of 18 files for every man, woman, and child in America. The U.S. Patent Office alone has 27 million documents on hand. While the Veterans Administration processes the files of 13.5 million veterans. The Department of Housing and Development keeps dossiers on 4.5 million Americans who have purchased homes through its federal home loan guarantee program (Magel, 199 1).

Corporate Databases

In the private sector, banks, insurance agencies, and credit rating agencies also process enormous volumes of computer data. For example, it is estimated that TRW Data Systems of California collects, stores and sells access information to the credit histories of more than 90 million Americans. Banks, department stores, jewelry stores, and credit card companies pay them a subscription fee to access such information on current and potential customers. More than 24,000 subscribers across the country use the TRW service. Likewise, every major insurance company in America collects and stores information on past, current, and future policy holders.

Telemarketing and mail-order professionals similarly buy, sell, and repackage such information like so many tangible products. The countless pieces of junk mail stuffed in Americans' mail boxes each day attest to the proliferation of such information brokers. Information brokers sell personal data to companies who then target for mail campaigns people who might be interested in their products. Information utilities such as CompuServe Information Service offer news and business bulletins, banking services, and an on-line encyclopedia. CompuServe alone has over 500,000 members accessing its 100 billion characters on on-line reviews of films, books, plays, and airline schedules from over 100 countries. The Dow Jones News-Retrieval Service offers stock market quotations, reports on business and economic forecasts plus profiles of companies and organizations. The Source not only provides news and stock market indexes but it also provides games and other forms of entertainment to its subscribers. Each of these information services is available to anyone with a computer, a modem, and a phone (Magel, 199 1).

AMERICA: A CASHLESS SOCIETY

The growth of the computer industry has also led to major changes in the way Americans handle money. Paper money is no longer necessary. It is estimated that over 90% of all business transactions involve the use of credit cards or checks (Fischer and Green, 1992-Rothman and Mosmann, 1985). Not only are computers used to process these documents, they also bill the customer's account and check on that customer's credit limit. If a credit card being used is over its credit limit or has been reported stolen or lost, the merchandiser knows immediately, and can stop the sale.

Point of sale systems (POS) add yet another dimension to this picture. With a POS, a store's cash register serves as a terminal to access a bank's computer. Instead of paying cash for an item or buying it on credit, the customer pays when the item is purchased by transferring funds directly from his or her account to that of the store (Rothman and Mosmann, 1985; Sawyer et al., 1995, Slotnick et al., 1986).

In addition, POS can lower business costs. For example, most checks take one to four days to clear the bank. The POS form of payment not only saves the business check processing charges, but also avoids the floating delay that follows all checking transactions (Rothman and

Mosmann, 1985). Conventional cash registers are 20% to 25% less expensive than POS systems, but POS systems can complete transaction in less than 40 seconds, instead of the nearly three minutes on a conventional cash register. POS systems produce detailed receipts for the customer, are more accurate, and cut employee training time. Finally, POS systems allow the number of check-out stations and personnel to be reduced by 25% to 50% (Slotnick et al., 1986).

Automatic teller machines (ATM) are typically small computers that function as terminals to a bank's central data-processing system. ATM's allow customers flexibility in withdrawing cash, checking their account balances, transferring funds between accounts, making deposits, and paying bills. This flexibility is due to ATM's being open twenty-four hours a day (Rothman and Mosmann, 1985).

Similarly, many banks allow customers to conduct financial transactions directly from home with the bank's computer by means of a computer or telephone. Bills can be paid or funds transferred from one account to another. Banking transactions are entered through the computer or telephone keypad by pressing keys for the account number, choosing the appropriate function, and receiving confirmation of the process (Magel, 1991).

A NATION OF ELECTRONIC PATHWAYS

Computer networks have likewise dramatically changed our society. The introduction of The Electronic Funds Transfer System has revolutionized the banking industry (EFTS). EFTS handles financial transactions through a wide-area computer network (WAN) rather than by exchanging cash. Banks, handling millions of checks a day, no longer mail them to the issuing bank to get reimbursed. They send electronic cash through the EFTS by automatically moving money from one bank to another regardless of its location. The Society of Worldwide Interbank Financial Telecommunications (SWIFT), the most sophisticated private interbank system in the world, averages 750,000 transactions daily for 13,000 member banks in 46 countries (Magel, 1991).

Electronic mail (E-MAIL) is a message delivery system using computers and communication channels to store and send mail. These channels travel over traditional telephone lines or through fiber optic cables. E-MAIL is non-simultaneous communications. Transmission and reception of E-MAIL occurs at different times, unlike a telephone call where one can hear and talk to another person simultaneously. E-MAIL automatically creates a permanent computer record of each transaction, unlike many other forms of communications (Sawyer et al., 1995; Slotnick et al., 1986).

THE NEED FOR COMPUTER SECURITY

A sharp increase in security-related problems has shadowed the expanding dependency of corporate and government agencies on computer technology and information storage. Computer crime statistics are showing an upward climb. A recent study of 236 major corporations (Zuckerman, 1996) reported the following findings involving computers:

- Approximately 58% of respondents suffered computer break-ins in the last year.

- Nearly 18% of companies reported computer-related losses greater than $1million.

- Two-thirds of the companies reported computer-related losses greater than $50,000.

- Hackers or competitors were responsible for almost 60% of the break-ins suffered by corporations.

- Approximately one-forth of the computer attacks sought trade secrets or documents of primary interest to a competitor.

Computer Crimes

In addition, approximately 66% of the companies surveyed caught employees making inappropriate use of company computer systems. Table I shows the losses that business suffered due to computer crimes.

Table I

Business Reporting Inappropriate use of Computer systems by the Dollar Amount Lost

Dollar Amount Lost	Inappropriate use by Insider/Employee	Inappropriate use by an Outsider
Unknown Amount	13%	21%
$0 - $1,000	0%	0%
$1,001 - $5,000	2%	0%
$5,001 - $10 , 000	5%	4%
$10,001 - $50,000	11%	8%
$50,001 - $200,000	22%	15%
$200,001 - $500,000	20%	19%
$500,001 - $1,000,000	11%	15%
Over $1,000,000	16%	18%

N = 236 (Parker, 1996)

As shown in Table 1, when the dollar amounts are less than $500,001, most of the inappropriate usage comes from employees. However when the dollar amount exceeds $500,001, outsiders are more likely to break into the computer system.

Most computer crimes reported in the news media focus on the sensational, headline grabbing cases. Examples include the Equity Funding Insurance Fraud and the Stanley Mark Rifkin story. Equity Funding Corporation of California and Illinois created over 70,000 false life insurance policies from 1967 to 1973 with a total value of $2.1 billion. In 1973, the fraud was discovered on a tip from a disgruntled employee and share holders lost over $600 million. In 1978, Stanley Mark Rifkin electronically transferred $10.2 million from the Security Pacific National Bank of California to Russia. Mr. Rifkin then used the stolen money to purchase 43,200 carats of Russian diamonds costing $8.145 million, which he intended to sell to a former business associate. The associate, upon discovering how Mr. Rifkin obtained the money, notified the FBI.

Stealing $5 million from a bank in North Carolina by fraudulently redirecting money from 3,000 individual savers' accounts to another bank employee's personal account generates considerable media interest, but stealing $1,000 from a small plumbing business in Colchester, Illinois by a similarly fraudulent method will undoubtedly be ignored by the media. Yet the resulting effect on the smaller business may ultimately be more damaging. Unfortunately, the type of crimes committed on a grand scale are often also perpetrated on the small scale. Those computer crimes that startled people a few years ago for their uniqueness and scope are now being offered in many communities across the nation (Magel, 1991). The following criminal acts typify offenses that have caused loss and continue to plague computer users.

During a Drug Enforcement Agency (DEA) probe in February of 1985, fake University of Southern California degrees were discovered. These counterfeit degrees where supported by false computer-stored transcripts. The degrees sold for $25,000 apiece (Carroll, 1996).

In July of 1985, seven youths were arrested in Plainfield, NJ. The juveniles had accessed unpublished Pentagon telephone numbers and ordered merchandise worth $1,000 on stolen credit card numbers (Carroll, 1996).

Apple Computer was victimized by a virus in December of 1987. The virus affected Apple's E-MAIL system, erasing all voice mail and shutting down the system. Criminals may have reverse-engineered the secret code that underlies Apple's Macintosh computers. This copyrighted code could be used to produce clones of the Macintosh computer (Icove, Seger, and VonStorch, 1996).

A West German programmer planted a "Trojan horse" program in IBM's E-MAIL system in December of 1987. The Trojan horse program displayed a holiday message, but if anyone tried to stop the message, E-MAIL and other information that had not been saved were lost. IBM had to shut down its computer system for 72 hours to purge the message (Icove et al., 1996).

In the communications industry, toll fraud is one of the oldest forms of computer crime and continues to be a concern. In February 1989, 15 inmates in the Davidson County Metro jails (Nashville, TN) were charged with accessing long-distance telephone accounts and charging over $2,000 in long-distance telephone charges in just one weekend (Icove et al., 1996).

Apparently in retaliation against articles written about crackers (people whose attacks on data systems have a malicious intent), two computer writers were the target of a "mail bomb." Someone in the fall of 1994 broke into the writers' Internet service provider (IBM and Sprint) and clogged their home computer mailbox with thousands of pieces of E-MAIL. This caused their Internet connection to shut down. The writers also had their home telephone numbers reprogrammed so that calls were forwarded to an out-of-state number. When a caller reached that number, an obscene recording was played (Icove et al., 1996).

In 1991, the FBI started Operation Innocent Images which focused on child pornography. During the investigation, Federal officials uncovered evidence that adults and juveniles were regularly using computers, linked through America Online and similar services, to transmit sexually explicit images of juveniles. In addition, adults were using the service to seek out minors for sexual encounters. Operation Innocent Images ended in 1995 with the arrest of more than a dozen customers of America Online (The News and Observer Publishing Co., 1995).

At the age of 17, Kevin Mitnick was convicted for breaking into Pacific Bell's and Digital Equipment Corporation (DEC) computers and served one year in prison. He was placed on parole in 1988. While on parole, Mitnick was accused of posing as a law enforcement officer to obtain sensitive Department of Motor Vehicle (DMV) information, stealing thousands of data files from computers, obtaining at least 20,000 credit card numbers from computers systems around the nation, and defrauding the cellular telecommunications industry out of millions of dollars for long distance service. Authorities believe that Mitnick broke into computers at Pacific Bell, the San Diego Supercomputer Center, Apple Computers Inc., and Motorola Inc.

These activities earned him the distinction of being the United States most wanted computer hacker. Kevin Mitnick was arrested by the FBI in February of 1995 for these alleged crimes and faced both federal and state criminal charges. On the twenty-three count federal indictment for telephone and computer fraud, Mitnick could have received 460 years in jail. By agreeing to plea guilty to one charge of cellular telephone fraud, Mitnick was sentenced to eight months (Littman, 1996; Shimomura and Markoff, 1996).

Randal Schwartz, a computer-programming expert, worked as a consultant for Intel Corporation. Mr. Schwartz was convicted in July 1995 in Superior Court for stealing passwords and making unauthorized changes in Intel's computer network. In this case the prosecutor asked the judge to order restitution of $60,000 to Intel (Computer expert convicted of hacking at Intel, 1995).

In February 1996, Jason Caine Anderson pleaded no contest to stealing five computer chips from Southern California Gas Company. The five stolen chips were valued at $2,400 (Associated Press, 1996).

Classic Methods for Committing Computer Crimes

Data Manipulation

Changing the data during or after input into a computer system is the simplest, safest, and most common method of committing computer crime. Any size of business is vulnerable to it. It can be performed by anyone associated with or having access to the processes for creating, recording, transporting, encoding, examining, checking, converting, or transforming the data that is eventually entered (Magel, 1991).

Salami Technique

This descriptive term implies trimming off small amounts of money from many sources and diverting these slices into one's own or an accomplice's account. This form of crime is most common in banking environments with their large number of savings and/or checking accounts and their automated financial processing. By creating a new program or altering an existing one, an employee can randomly deduct one to five cents from a few thousand different individual accounts. The accumulated sums can then be withdrawn by normal methods from his or her receiving account (Magel, 199 1).

Trojan Horse

Appropriately named after the hollow horse given to the city of Troy, Trojan Horse programs seem legitimate. These programs will behave as if it is and will do what the computer operator expects. However, the Trojan Horse contains either a block of undesired computer code or another computer program that allows the Trojan Horse program to do things detrimental to the system that the operator is not aware of--such as infecting a machine with a virus, worm, bomb, or trap door. Remember, a Trojan Horse program appears innocent and attracts users by inviting them to load it as some type of software. In reality, Trojan Horse programs are not software, but a ruse designed to penetrate a computer system so that a program of the penetrator's choosing can become active (Carroll, 1996; Levine, 1995; Sawyer et al., 1995-, Simonds, 1996).

Viruses

According to the popular press and the world in general, a virus is any hidden computer code that copies itself to other programs. In the computer field, a virus is a set of unwanted instructions executed on a computer resulting in a variety of effects. Presently there are approximately 500 core viruses and about 3,000 variations. The term "virus disruption" is used to categorize computer viruses (Carroll, 1996; Dunham, 1996; Levine, 1995; Sawyer et al., 1995; Simonds, 1996).

Viruses fall into one of four categories based on the type of damage that the virus inflicts. Innocuous viruses cause no noticeable disruption or destruction with the computer system. When humorous text or a graphic message is displayed without causing any damage or loss of data, then a humorous virus has infected the system. Categories three and four cause damage to the data stored in the computer system. Altering viruses change system data subtlety (e.g., moving a decimal to a different place, adding or deleting a digit). When sudden widespread destruction of data both on the computer system and on peripheral devices occurs, the machine is possibility infected with a catastrophic virus (Levine, 1995).

Worms

Some people regard worms and viruses as the same type of program. Each has a replication mechanism, an activation mechanism, and an objective. Nevertheless, viruses and worms are very different kinds of programs. While viruses just infect programs, worms take over computer memory and deny its use to legitimate programs (Levine, 1995; Losey, 1996; Simonds, 1996).

Hostile Applets

A new danger exists when using the World Wide Web (YAW) to obtain information. The danger is from so-called hostile applets that utilize a Java-enabled Web page. Java is Sun Microsystems' scripting language. Just as viruses perform a variety of tasks without the user's knowledge, so do hostile applets. The effects can range from mild distraction to data loss (Hoffman, 1996).

Bombs

Like the Trojan horse method, a bomb is a computer code inserted by a programmer into legitimate software. There are two types of bombs: time bombs and logic bombs. A date or time triggers a time bomb, whereas some event, perhaps the copying of a file, triggers a logic bomb. There are several advantages to using bombs. The built in delay makes the program harder to trace. Perpetrators can plan the event for maximum effect, with the delay allowing the bomb to be copied into backup files. Also, some companies implant bombs in their software. If customers fall behind in payments, or if customers attempt to copy the program, the bomb is set off and the program stops or the system is halted (Carroll, 1996; Levine, 1995; Sawyer et al., 1995; Simonds, 1996; Slotnick et al., 1986).

Trap and Back Doors

Doors allow programmers extensive access to test systems while they are being developed, allowing programmers access that would normally be denied. There are two types: trap doors and back doors. Trap doors are intentionally created and are normally inserted during software development. These doors are supposed to be removed once the software is completed. Unintentional access to software code is referred to as a back door (Levine, 1995; Simonds, 1996).

Time Stealing

This is one of the most common forms of computer crime because people do not consider the cost of accessing a computer without authorization. Any access uses the computer's resources (hardware, memory, software, peripherals) which cost money. Time stealing is comparable to driving another person's car without their knowledge (Magel, 1991).

Electronic Eavesdropping

Tapping, without authorization, into communication lines over which digitized computer data and messages are being sent is electronic eavesdropping. By using technologically advanced listening devices, eavesdropping can be performed on traditional telephone lines and even satellite transmission networks. If data transmitted are not encoded, capturing and transforming the data is equivalent to using a clandestine tape recorder to record a standard telephone conversation (Magel, 1991).

Software Piracy

Providing software for computers is big business. Software programs can cost from a few dollars to thousands of dollars. Because of this, some people are willing to copy software and resell or give it away. This unauthorized coping of copyrighted, marketable or nonmarketable computer programs is referred to as software piracy. It has been estimated that for each legitimate copy of a software package sold, between 4 and 30 additional copies are made illegally. Although most copied programs are not resold, they deny vendors and software developers profits that should have accrued legally (Rothman and Mosmann, 1985; Sawyer et al., 1995; Slotnick et al., 1986).

COMPUTER SYSTEMS PROTECTION

Security professionals must protect information contained within the computer system from damage or loss. The system might contain any of the following components: an electronic data processing (EDP) center, local area networks (LAN), wide area networks (WAN), or a PC. Regardless of the type of system, the security professional's dilemma is how to balance convenience of using the system against protecting the system from disasters, systems failures, or unauthorized access. Disaster-recovery planning, identification and access of software and data control, encryption, and physical security are the four facets of computer protection (Sawyer et al., 1995).

Disaster-Recovery Planning

Disasters such as fires, floods, and earthquakes are potential hazards to essential computer systems. Because these threats are unpredictable, businesses must develop contingency or disaster-recovery plans. Contingency planning requires more than an occasional emergency drill. Plans must cover all business functions, including but not limited to, emergency response requirements, personnel resources, hardware backup, software and data file backup, and backup for related and special activities (Hutt, 1995; Sawyer et al., 1995).

Contingency Procedures

Every company should have procedures for dealing with emergencies, whether natural or man-made. Without such planning, the initial response might be a "knee-jerk" reaction which could lead to people being injured or killed and damage or destruction of data, software, and hardware. To guard against counterproductive "knee-jerk" reactions, companies must implement contingency planning. Prior comprehensive planning is the first line of defense against disasters (Hutt, 1995).

Placing, the Computer Center. As a rule computer centers should not be in a basement, below-grade-level, or on first-floor sites. This prevents the entry of surface water into the center. In addition to avoiding areas that are prone to flooding, computer centers should not be placed in sites along known geological fault lines. If this is not possible, make sure that the building is constructed using approved earthquake-proof practices (Carroll, 1996).

Certain areas of any building present problems for security. First-floor sites are most vulnerable to forcible attack, surreptitious intrusion, civil commotion, or terrorist attack. The top floor also presents opportunities for illegal activities. People can enter the facility through skylights or by cutting through the roof.

Ideally, from a security standpoint, computer centers should be within a company-owned area at least 200 feet from the closest public access. If the building houses other types of business, then the computer center should be on a floor completely occupied by the company and the floor above and below the site should also be company occupied. If a new site is being selected, the preferred location is either rural or suburban (Carroll, 1996).

Fire Protection. Buildings housing computer centers should be of noncombustible construction to reduce the chance of fire. These facilities must be continuously monitored for temperature, humidity, water leaks, smoke, and fire. Most building codes today require that sprinkler systems be installed.

Remember that water and electrical equipment do not mix. It is preferable to install a dry pipe sprinkler system rather than a wet pipe system. Dry pipe systems only allow water into the pipes after heat is sensed. This avoids potential wet pipe problems, such as leakage. In addition, fast-acting sensors can be installed to shut down electricity before water sprinklers are activated. Sprinkler heads should be individually activated to avoid wide-spread water damage.

Another type of fire suppression system uses chemicals instead of water. The two approved types of chemical were Halon 1301 (also known as Freon 12) and FM-200. Halon systems are still in common use, but the chemical itself was banned in 1994 by the United Nations because it contributes to destruction of the ozone layer in the upper atmosphere. Once this system is utilized it must be recharged with either recycled Halon, or the fire system must be slightly modified and FM-200 installed. FM-200 is similar to Halon, but with no atmospheric ozone depleting potential. Carbon dioxide flooding systems are also available, but should never be used Carbon dioxide suffocates fire by removing the oxygen from the room. While this effectively extinguishes most fires, it also suffocates people still in the effected area.

All chemical fire suppression systems are relatively expensive and require long and complex governmental approval to install. Neither chemical fire suppression system protects people from smoke inhalation, nor can they deal effectively with electrical fires. They are, however, the only fire suppression system that does not require computer equipment to be turned off, assuring the quickest possible return to normal operations.

Regarding fire extinguishers, there should be at least one 10-pound fire extinguisher within 50 feet of every equipment cabinet. Also at least one 5-pound fire extinguisher should be installed for people who are unable to handle the larger units. These extinguishers should be filled with either Halon, FM-200, or carbon dioxide. None of these agents require special clean up.

Install at least one water-filled pump-type fire extinguisher to use for extinguishing minor paper fires. Employees should be trained and constantly reminded not to use water extinguishers on electrical equipment because of the possibility of electric shock to personnel and damage to the equipment. They should also be discouraged from using foam, dry chemicals, acid-water, or soda water extinguishers. The first two are hard to remove and the others are caustic and will damage computer components (Carroll, 1996; Platt, 1995).

Personnel Issues

Crisis management focuses on the swift and effective action of personnel. This means that anyone involved in the emergency response plan must be adequately trained and kept up to date on any changes in procedures. When ranking emergency response procedures, protection of life is the most important, followed by protection of property, and finally limitation of damage. One way to verify that employees are familiar and have current knowledge of the contingency plan is to conduct periodic drills (Carroll, 1996; Hutt, 1995).

Hardware Backup

Most people think contingency planning and hardware backup as the same thing. This is not the case. Hardware backup is only one element of contingency planning. In this phase, classifying possible disruptions is useful so that hardware backup strategies can be developed. There are three categories of disruptions: nondisasters, disasters, and catastrophes (Hutt, 1995).

"Nondisaster" disruptions are normally system malfunctions or other failures. Disasters cause the entire facility to be inoperative for longer than one day. Catastrophes entail the destruction of the data processing facility. In this last category, a new facility must be built or an existing alternate structure must be identified to be used as the computer center (Hutt, 1995).

Once the extent of the disruption is ascertained, the company must make arrangements for alternate locations to conduct their computer operations. Alternative locations are categorized into hot, warm, and cold sites. Hot sites are fully configured and ready to operate within several hours. Warm sites are partially configured, but are missing the central computer. Because the central computer is missing, these sites are less expensive than hot sites. However, warm sites may take several days or weeks to locate and install the main computer and any other missing equipment. Once the equipment is installed, these sites can be operational within several hours. The least expensive sites are referred to as "cold" sites. These locations are ready to receive the equipment but do not have any components installed in advance. Cold sites take at least several weeks to become operational (Hutt, 1995; Sawyer et al., 1995).

The major distinctions in choosing the right "temperature" of the three types of sites are the company's needs in terms of activation time and cost. All companies must also have a way of alerting personnel of a disruption and telling employees which site to report to for work. Computer personnel must also be trained to operate the hardware at the new site. Finally, the hardware must be compatible with the equipment that was damaged or destroyed (Hutt, 1995; Sawyer et al., 1995).

Software and Information Backup

Software includes operating systems (e.g., DOS, Windows, Unix, etc.), programming languages (e.g., C, Pascal, Ada, COBOL, etc.), utilities (virus checkers, security programs, batch files, etc.), and application programs (word processors, data bases, accounting programs, etc.). Keep in mind, if the hardware at the alternate site is not compatible with the computers at the company, then the software will not operate (e.g., trying to run MAC programs on an IBM computer).

Information and software are less tangible and more dynamic than hardware. For protecting these elements, it is necessary to consider both the physical storage environment and the frequency of change in data. Backing up information and software can protect the company from loss. Regardless of the approach used, backing up data involves copying files onto machine readable media. The backup media can be tapes, floppy disks, hard drives, or CD-ROMS (Hutt, 1995).

Information and software should be stored at on- and off-site locations. Many large organizations employ a tiered strategy, employing several levels of backups to achieve a balance of safety and convenience. Ideally, a business should have four sets of backup files with one set of files staying on-site and three sets of files being stored off-site.

On-site files should be housed in a fire-resistant safe designed for computer media. These files are the most recently created backup files until replaced by newer generations. Next, there is an off-site local backup location. This location is normally within a half-mile radius of the computer site. Files at this site are stored in a fire-resistant vault and accessed daily for rotation. Backup files are retained there for one week. Once files leave the off-site local storage facility, then they are moved to an off-site remote location, which is a minimum of five miles from the computer center. This site also contains a fire-resistant vault designed for computer media and is accessed weekly. The remote location is used to retain remaining backup files in active use for more than one week. Finally, any permanent records that need to be retained for several years are removed to archival storage. Archival facilities should be more than 50 miles away from the original computer site. The vault should be fire-resistant and earthquake-resistant. From the security standpoint, as the storage facility becomes more remote, accessibility decreases and security increases (Hutt, 1995).

Backup for Related and Special Activities

Besides protecting computer hardware and software, source documents must be protected. Source documents contain information transformed into machine-readable data from which printouts are generated. The printouts are referred to as either human-readable output or hard copies. This output is used to assist in furthering business activities of the organization. Source documents should be copied or backed-up in the event of loss or destruction so that the basic information can be reconstructed in an emergency. Backing up may take the form of duplicate copies, photocopies, microfilm, microfiche, or other media (Hutt, 1995).

Identification and Access of Software and Data

People used to believe that only highly skilled technicians could gain access to computers. This illusion has been shattered by many well-publicized news stories. Today many people believe that any individual possessing basic computer skills can break into a computer system. Because of this perception and the fact that it has occasionally been proven correct, organizations must now go to tremendous lengths to protect their software and data (Sawyer et al., 1995; Walsh, 1995).

Computer systems can use three methods to determine if a person has a legitimate right to access the system. The three categories are:

- What a person has--cards, keys, and badges

- What a person knows--personal identification numbers (PINs), passwords, and digital signatures

- Who a person is--physical traits

Each of these authentication methods are designed to make impersonation difficult (Kabay, 1995-, Sawyer et al., 1995).

What a person has

Some systems require that an employee insert cards, a key, or a badge into the machine before it will allow access to data. Credit cards, debit cards, cash-machine cards, and badges are examples of cards. Cards can contain either a magnetic strip or a computer chip. Cards containing a computer chip are referred to as "smart" cards. With this card, the operator must insert the card before the machine will allow that person to access any information. With a keylock system, a person must unlock the computer to use the system. This is one of the most popular types of security features found on PCS . Most PCS have a key-lock installed that allows the authorized user to "lock out" the keyboard. When the system is "locked," keyboard input is not recognized (Bologna, 1995; Kabay, 1995; Sawyer et al., 1995).

Cards, keys, or badges can be lost, stolen, or counterfeited (Kabay, 1995; Sawyer et al., 1995). In addition, the key-locks on PCS can be disabled if a person can remove the case of the machine. This drastic method is seldom necessary, as most PC locks use the same type of key. If someone has a computer with a key-lock, then it is possible that his or her key can open or close the lock on the unauthorized computer.

What a person knows

PINS, passwords, and digital signatures fall under this category. These security features work with any computer system. PINs work in conjunction with various types of card systems (e.g., ATM cards or phone cards). With this system one inserts a card and then enters the PIN. The PIN is a security number known only to the user. Passwords are special words, codes, or symbols required to access a computer system. Passwords work in conjunction with access logs. Access logs keeps track of who got in, how many times they tried to enter, when they entered (date, time, and even location), and when they left, whereas passwords allow an operator into the system. To discourage the misuse of passwords, companies should require passwords to contain at least eight characters which could be any combination of symbols, capital and lowercase letters, and numbers. Easily guessed or obvious passwords should be discouraged. Finally, the company may assign passwords to employees that are meaningless numbers, letters, or both. If the system requires a high degree of security, then a password should only be used once. The last "what a person knows" category, digital signatures, is relatively new. This system uses a public-private key system. One person creates the signature with a secret private key, and the receiver reads it with a second, public key. The "signature" is a string of characters and numbers that a user signs to an electronic document (Carroll, 1996; David, 1995; Hoyt, 1995; Kabay, 1995; Sawyer et al., 1995; Slotnick et al., 1986).

The two biggest pitfalls of the "knows" systems are associated with passwords and PINS. Passwords can be guessed. People have a tendency to use real words (e.g., their name, birth date, friends' or childrens' names, user initials, social security numbers, etc.). Some system operators even fail to replace the default password. PINs and passwords are frequently written down by employees in convenient places easily discovered by others (David, 1995; Hoyt, 1995; Kabay, 1995; Sawyer et al., 1995).

Who a person is

Biometric methods are utilized in this category. Biometrics encompass the science of measuring individual body characteristics. Fingerprints, hand geometry, retinal patterns, voice recognition, keystroke dynamics, signature dynamics, and lip prints are common methods used to identify authorized users. In each of these methods, the computer compares the item being scanned with a copy of the item stored in the computer's memory. If the compared items match, the computer allows access. If not, the person is denied entry. Biometric techniques are not usually found on PCS because they require expensive equipment to be connected to the computer. This equipment limits mobility, which restricts its use with portable computers (Kabay, 1995; Sawyer eta]., 1995) .

Encryption

The best way to protect any type of data is to encrypt it. This also happens to be one of the best ways to protect data on portable machines, like laptop computers. Encryption "scrambles" the information so that it is not usable unless the changes are reversed. Today there are at least five different methods for encrypting data. Data Encryption Standard (DES) is a 56-bit algorithm. This standard was first published in 1977, and is used to protect Federal unclassified information (in this usage, unclassified means sensitive information not falling with "top secret" parameters). It has been adopted by commercial users. DES is used on financial applications to protect electronic fund transfers and by the Internet to encrypt information. In 1978, a 512-bit key was developed that uses the Rivest, Shamir, and Adleman (RSA) algorithm. Another encryption algorithm is Pretty Good Privacy (PGP). Using both the International Data Encryption algorithm (IDEA) and RSA algorithms, this product is available over the Internet and has become somewhat of a defacto standard for encryption on the Internet. A new algorithm called Skipjack has been developed by the National Security Agency (NSA) to replace DES. Placed in a computer chip, this algorithm is referred to as a clipper chip. An enhanced Clipper chipset is called Capstone. These chips allow law enforcement and other agencies with access to the algorithm key to break the encrypted information. The Communications Assistance for Law Enforcement Act (CALEA) preserves law enforcement ability, pursuant to court order or other lawful authorization, to access communications and associated call-identifying information. CALEA mandates that law enforcement agencies have the legal right to break encryption algorithms. One last system utilizes both encryption and digital signatures to protect e-mail. This system is called Privacy Enhanced Mail (PEM). PEM uses both DES and RSA algorithms to encrypt e-mail messages. (Freeh, 1996;Levine, 1995; Rothfeder, 1996; Simonds, 1996; Sussman, 1995).

Physical Security

Physical security places barriers in the path of attackers to deter them from attacking, delay them if they decide to attack, and deny them access to high-value targets should they succeed in penetrating the security system. There are two methods of security planning: traditional planning and strategic planning. Traditional methods start from the outside perimeter and work inward, whereas strategic methods are applied in just the opposite way (National Crime Prevention Institute[NCPI], 1986).

Electronic Data Processing Centers

Electronic data processing centers (EDP) have the same physical security needs as do any businesses or industrial establishments. Most EDP centers use the traditional security approach, beginning with the protection of the grounds around the building, then proceeding to the building's perimeter, the building's interior, and the contents of the building (Fischer and Green, 1992; NCPI, 1986).

With an EDP center, the outer shell provides perimeter protection and includes walls, fences, or partitions. Entrance protection restricts entry points to the EDP center. Doors and other entry points should be restricted to locations essential for safe evacuation in an emergency. A receptionist or security officer should be stationed at each entry point during all hours that the department is working.

Compartmentalizing a computer center into clearly defined rooms according to function (control, central processor, test and maintenance, storage, media library, forms, printing, waste) provides additional security. It enables access to each area to be controlled and restricted to authorized personnel. Electronic access control mechanisms such as badge reading locks should be only issued to personnel with a need to be in a given area. These badges can also be time stamped to restrict access to authorized times.

In all circumstances, the computer room should be limited to operations personnel. Protection of these critical areas should follow the principle of "Authorized Access Only." Only those persons specifically necessary to its operation are allowed into the computer room. This should be the only room where programs, data, and computer equipment are all brought together extremely tight control of this room is imperative if the integrity and confidentiality of the data and programs are to be preserved. Installation of detection intrusion devices to monitor these critical areas when not occupied is warranted. These devices are usually wired directly to the department or company security office station to alert, identify, and monitor the location of an intruder (Magel, 199 1).

Personal Computers

Security used to be much easier when we only had EDP centers. These centers were and still are centralized, containing mainframe or super computers. Today, there are a multitude of personal computer systems. These systems range from mini computers to pocket PCS. In addition, many of these stand-alone PCS are connected together to form either LANs or WANS. Furthermore, the user community is mobile and needs access to ever-increasing on-line resources (Simonds, 1996). Because of this, traditional security methods are inappropriate and inadequate. To protect PCS, the strategic method, where protection starts from the computer and works toward the perimeter, is best (NCPI, 1986).

A company's personal computers, like all other corporate computers, should have access limited to authorized users only. If all the computers are in a central location, restrict entry to this area using methods similar to the security measures used in EDP centers.

With LAN systems, begin security procedures by locking up everything that can be physically secured. With the strong trend toward concentrating control of LANs at hubs, the LAN system becomes increasingly vulnerable. Make sure that the wiring closets are secured with an appropriate lock system. Another entry point for obtaining data from an LAN system is through the wiring itself. In most companies, the wiring is hidden in the ceiling, walls, or under the carpet, giving a wiretapper a choice of points of entry. All original, necessary wiring needs to be documented and diagrammed. By routinely checking the diagrams against existing wiring, new or suspicious additions will alert security to a potential problem (Simonds, 1996).

For any PCS placed on a person's desk, a lockdown system attaching the equipment to the desk must be installed. There are four types of lockdown systems: cages, plates, cables, and alarms. These various systems discourage theft of the equipment. Do not neglect to ensure that equipment covers are tamper resistant. Some criminals are now removing computer chips taken from inside computers' cases and reselling them (Carroll, 1996; David, 1995).

In a similar vein, portable computers have become a popular item to steal. In 1995 over 200,000 of these thefts were reported. During the Gulf War, a lap-top computer was stolen from a military staff officer's automobile in England. This machine's hard drive contained detailed plans for Great Britain's participation in the war. A common scam in many hotels, motels, and airports, is for a person in front of the person with the portable computer to slow the line down. If the target puts the notebook computer down, an accomplice standing behind the intended victim picks up the notebook and walks away. The first line of defense against that theft is "street smarts." This basically means keeping the computer in one's constant physical possession (Carroll, 1996; Stone, 1996).

Besides protecting the computer itself, security must also be concerned with the storage media (i.e., floppies, tapes, etc.). People do transport storage media between work and home even if company police forbids the practice. Floppies and computer tape cassettes are small enough to fit into a shirt pocket. Even if the work environment is secure, the home environment is not. Media can also be lost between work and home. If the information contained is sensitive or irreplaceable data or programs, such a loss could be catastrophic. Employees can also alter the data, taking it back to the office where it is used to update the central computer. This incorrect data would then impact the entire organization (Simonds, 1996).

LEGAL ISSUES AND LEGISLATION

Before 1978, authorities had to rely on traditional statutes (i.e., mail and wire fraud, larceny, theft of services, embezzlement, trespass, and destruction of property) to prosecute individuals committing forms of computer abuse. New crimes often do not fit the parameters of the preexisting legal framework (i.e., money siphoned off using "salami" frauds or files may be stolen even though the owner still retains copies, etc.). To deal with these "new" categories of crime, Florida passed the first computer crime law in 1978 (Carroll, 1996; Rasch, 1996)

State Legislation

Since the passing of Florida's original computer crime law, every state with the exception of Vermont has enacted similar legislation. Many of these statutes are based on the federal computer Fraud and Abuse Act of 1986. Definitions of computers, computer systems, computer networks, computer supplies, data, and other fundamental terms still vary widely from state to state (Carroll, 1996; Rasch, 1996).

Federal Legislation

The Computer Fraud and Abuse Act of 1986 (CFAA) was the first truly comprehensive federal computer crime statute and was an extension of Federal statute 18 U.S.C. 1030 which was enacted in 1984. The CFAA has been amended in 1986, 1988, 1989, and 1990. This law only covers federal "interest" computers. A federal interest computer is one owned, leased, or operated by or for the federal government, contains federally protected information, or is used in interstate commerce (Carroll, 1996; Rasch, 1996).

This Act contemplates six offenses: the unauthorized access of a computer to obtain information of national security with an intent to injure the United States or give advantage to a foreign nation; the unauthorized access of a computer to obtain protected financial or credit information; the unauthorized access into a computer used by the federal government; the unauthorized interstate or foreign access of a computer system with an intent to defraud; the unauthorized interstate or foreign access of computer systems that results in at least $1,000 aggregate damage or modifies or impairs medical records; and the fraudulent trafficking in computer passwords affecting interstate commerce. Penalties range from $5,000 to $100,000 or two times the value obtained by the offense, whichever is higher, or imprisonment from 1 to 20 years or both. These violations are investigated by the FBI's National Computer Crime Squad (NCCS). The NCCS was authorized by the CFAA. (Carroll, 1996; FBI-NCCS, 1996; Rasch, 1996).

The Computer Fraud and Abuse Act covers all phases of computer crime including hacking, misuse of passwords, and bulletin boards. Electronic trespassers now commit a felony when they enter a federally related computer with intent to defraud. The "malicious damage" felony violation applies to any hacker altering information in that computer. Preventing other legal users from accessing the computer is also defined as a felony.

The CFAA has a far reaching new provision regarding electronic bulletin boards. It is now a misdemeanor for any bulletin board operator to provide "any password or similar information through which a computer may be accessed without authorization." This includes any sharing of information with other board users on how to break into computers (Magel, 1991).

Copyright Laws

The federal Copyright Act protects the way words and computer code are expressed but not the ideas themselves. Copyright begins at the moment the source code or the manual is written and belongs to the employer. Care must be taken when programs or manuals are prepared by an outside consultant to ensure that the company retains the copyright on these products by way of contract (Bigelow, 1995; Carroll, 1996).

Before 1989, the law required that a copyright notice be included before a work was published (i.e., offered for sale or voluntarily disclosed). Failure to include the copyright notice could result in loss of copyright protection. However, on March 1, 1989 this law changed. The United States became a party to the Beme Copyright Convention. Today, the copyright notice is no longer required for protection. Nevertheless, it is still advisable in any document that will be widely distributed to include the copyright notice. This inclusion makes it much more difficult for an infringer to plead innocence or ignorance (Bigelow, 1995a).

License Agreements

Contract law has also been used to protect computer software or data. By specific contract with each purchaser, the program developer grants the program users a right to use the program. This is called a license agreement. A license is distinguished from a sale. Under license, the program users do not own the software; they simply have the right to use it as it was designed. Many previously enacted criminal laws rely on the concept of authorized or permitted use. In an attempt to protect their software, developers often depend on the tenets of contract law (Magel, 1991).

Trade Secret Law

Other software houses rely on trade secret law. A trade secret is information that gives one company a competitive edge over other companies. Soft drink formulas, fried chicken recipes, the chemical composition of the Stealth Bomber's fuselage are all examples of trade secrets. Trade secret protection allows distribution of the results of a secret while keeping the specifics of its design hidden. In relation to computer software, under trade secret law, it is illegal to steal a secret algorithm and use it in another company's program. In order for trade secret law to be effective. Employees who have access to the secret must be required not to divulge the secret and the owner must take precautions to guard against its disclosure (Magel, 1991).

Privacy Legislation

The federal government has over 2,000 databases with personal information. States and private businesses have databases numbering in the thousands also containing personal information. Since most data currently used by State and Federal government agencies also is gathered, stored, organized, or processed by means of computers, there are several federal statutes controlling its use. In total, these laws attempt to limit the number of assaults on personal and corporate privacy (Bigelow, 1995b).

In 1970 the United States Congress passed the Freedom of Information Act allowing citizens to find out which Federal agencies keep records on them. They are also permitted to secure copies of the records to verify their accuracy. The Fair Credit Reporting Act of 1970 gave people the right to inspect their credit rating records. Credit agencies holding computer records are legally required to investigate the accuracy of that data. In 1973, the Crime Control Act was passed. This Act requires that when arrest histories are distributed, the data must show not only that an arrest took place, but whether or not prosecution and conviction followed. The Privacy Act of 1974 protects the privacy of personal data collected for one purpose from being used for another without the individual's consent; it gives people the right to discover what information the government has collected about them; it allows individuals to have copies of their files; and it provides a way for people to correct inaccurate data. The Family Educational Rights and Privacy Act of 1974 restricts access to computer records of grades and behavior evaluations in private and public schools. Under this statute, students also have the right to examine and challenge the accuracy of the data in their records. In 1988, the Computer Matching and Privacy Protection Act was enacted, regulating "computer matching." Computer matching uses data processing techniques to compare records of payments to individuals receiving pay, benefits, or both from different governmental agencies. If, for example, a person was discovered getting welfare benefits, yet also has records with the IRS reflecting a $45,000 annual income, the government could instantly start penalizing the individual. Under this Act, individuals are given a chance to respond to allegations before the federal government is allowed to take adverse actions against them. The Act also prohibits disclosure of personal records unless the disclosure falls under one of 12 exceptions. Examples of exceptions permitting disclosure include agencies making matching discoveries during "routine use" of data and computer matches generated for law enforcement or tax purposes (Bigelow, 1995b, Magel, 1991, Sawyer et al., 1995).

Financial Privacy

Several other laws focus on financial privacy. The Tax Reform Act of 1976 puts boundaries on the Internal Revenue Service, limiting its access to personal information in bank records. It also restricts that agency from circulating its data to other government agencies. In 1978, the Right to Financial Privacy Act was passed. It establishes regulations on government access to customer files in financial institutions, and gives citizens the right to examine the data contained in their own financial files. The Debt Collection Act of 1982 sets up due-process conditions which federal agencies must follow before releasing any information about an individual's bad debts to credit bureaus. As a result of the Cable Communication Policy Act of 1984, cable television services must inform their customers if any personal information about them is being collected, used or disclosed to any government or corporate agency (Magel, 1991; Sawyer et al., 1995).

The above sampling of Federal and State legislation shows how American institutions are adapting to the increasing number of computer related abuses.

REFERENCES

Bigelow, R. P. 1995a. Legal issues in computer security. In A. E. Hutt, S. Bosworth, & D. B. Hoyt (Eds.) Computer security handbook (3 d ed; pp 5.1 -5.29). New York: John Wiley & Sons.

Bigelow, R. P. 1995b. Computer privacy in the United States. In A. E. Hutt, S. Bosworth, & D. B. Hoyt (Eds.) Computer security handbook (3" ed; pp II. I - II. 14). New York: John Wiley & Sons.

Bologna, G. J. 1995. Computer crime and computer criminals. In A. E. Hutt, S. Bosworth, & D. B. Hoyt (Eds.) Computer securitv handbook (3' ed; pp 6.1 -6.3 1). New York: John Wiley & Sons.

Carroll, J. M. 1996. Computer security (3ded). Boston: Butterworth-Heinemann.

Computer expert convicted of hacking at Intel 1995. [On-line].
Http://www.sjmercury.com/speciaVreprint/randal2.htm

Covington, P. A. 1991. Computers: the plain Enylish guide (3' ed). Jackson, Michigan: QNS Publishing.

David, J. R. 1995. Security for personal computers. In A. E. Hutt, S. Bosworth, & D.B. Hoyt (Eds.) Computer security (3d ed.; pp 21.1 - 21.21). New York: John Wiley & Sons.

Dunham, K. 1996. Introduction to viruses. [On-line].
Http:Hwww.iste.org/-iste/antivirus/intro.htm

Federal Bureau of Investigation 1996, February 7. Information concerning implementation of the Communications Assistance for Law Enforcement Act (CALEA) [On-line].
Http://www.fbi.gov/congress/telecom/leahy.htm

Federal Bureau of Investigation's Criminal Justice Information Services Division 1996. [On-line]. Http:Hwww.fbi.gov/over/services.htm#cjis

Federal Bureau of Investigation National Computer Crime Squad 1996. [On-line].
Http://www.fbi.gov/compcrim.htm

Fischer, R. J. & Green, G. (1992). Introduction to security 5' ed.. Boston: Butterworth-Heinemann.

Freeh, L. J. 1996, July 25. Impact of encryption on law enforcement and public safety [On-line]. Http://www.fbi.gov/congress/encrypt/encrypt.htm

Hoffman, H. 1996, October. Hostile applets: The dark side of Java. Computer Shopper, p.80.

Hoyt, D. B. 1995. Security of computer data, records, and forms. In A. E. Hutt, S. Bosworth, & D. B. Hoyt (Eds.) Computer security (3d ed.; pp 15.1 - 15.24). New York: John Wiley & Sons.

Hutt, A. E. 1995. Contingency planning and disaster recovery. In A. E. Hutt, S. Bosworth, & D. B. Hoyt (Eds.) Computer security handbook (3' ed; pp 7.1 - 7.35). New York: John Wiley & Sons.

IAFIS: The real story 1996. [On-line]. Http://www.fbi.gov/IAFIS/story.htm

Icove,   D., Seger, K., & VonStorch, W. 1996. Fightiny Computer Crime. [On-line]. Http://www.cs.nsu.edu:80/others/seminar/notes/crimel.htmi

Kabay, M. E. 1995. Penetrating computer systems and networks. In A. E. Hutt, S. Bosworth, & D.   B. Hoyt (Eds.), Computer security handbook (3d; pp 18.1 - 18.22).

Levine, D. E. 1995. Viruses and related threats to computer security. In A. E. Hutt, S. Bosworth, & D. B. Hoyt (Eds.), Computer security handbook (3d ed; pp 19.1 - 19.24), New York: John Wiley & Sons.

Littman, J. 1996. The fugitive game: Online with Kevin Mitnick. Boston: Little, Brown, and Co.

Mackall, K. 1996a, February. NCIC 2000 - Linking it all together. NCIC 2000 Newsletter 1(1) [On-line]. Available: http://www.fbi.gov/2000/2kvlnl.htm

Mackall, K. 1996b, Apri/May. NCIC 2000- Linking it all together. NCIC 2000 Newsletter, 1(3) [On-line]. Available: http:Hwww.fbi.gov/2000/2kvln3.htm

Magel, T. 1991. Computer security. In J. Chuvala & R. J. Fischer (Eds.), Suggested preparation for careers in security/loss prevention (pp 103 - 120). Dubuque, Iowa. Kendall/Hunt.

National Crime Prevention Institute 1986. Understanding crime prevention. Boston: Butterworths.

Parker, S. 1996, November 21. Computer crime scene. USA Today, p. B4.

Platt, F. N. 1995. Computer facility protection. In A. E. Hutt, S. Bosworth, & D. B. Hoyt (Eds.), Computer security handbook (3' ed; pp 12.1-12.24). New York: John Wiley & Sons.

Rasch, M. D. 1996. Legal lessons in the computer age. [On-line]. Http://www. securitymanagement.conVlibrary/000 I 22.html

Rothfeder, J. 1996, November. Hacked! Are your company files safe? PC World 170-182.

Rothman, S. & Mosmann, C. 1985. Computer uses and issues. Chicago: Science Research Associates.

Sawyer, S. C., Williams, B. K., & Hutchinson, S. E. 1995. Using information technology: A practical introduction to computers and communications (Brief Ed.). Chicago: Irwin.

Shimomura, T. & Markoff, J. 1996. Takedown: The pursuit and capture of Kevin Mitnick, America's most wanted computer outlaw--by the man who did it. New York: Hyperion.

Simonds, F. 1996. Network Security: Data and voice communications. New York: McGraw Hill.

Slotnick, D. L., Butterfield, E. M., Kopetzky, D. J., & Slotnick, J. K. 1986. Computers and applications: An introduction to data processing. Lexington, Massachusetts: D.C. Health and Co.

Stone, M. D. 1996, December. Gone before it's time: Guarding against notebook theft. Computer Shopper, 340-341.

Sussman, V. 1995, January 23. Policing cyberspace. U.S. News & World Report, 55-60.

Walsh, M. E. 1995. Software and information security. In A. E. Hutt, S. Bosworth, & D. B. Hoyt (Eds.), Computer security handbook (3 d ed; pp. 14.1-14.20). New York: John Wiley & Sons.

Zuckerman, M. J. 1996, November 21. Cybercrime against business frequent, costly. USA Today pp. Al, B4.

CHAPTER 10

FIRE SCIENCE AND EMERGENCY PROCEDURES

Don Bytner, Chief
Macomb Illinois Fire Department

Explanation is given as to why knowledge of fire suppression techniques is necessary for loss prevention personnel. Aside from trying to prevent losses and injury, some of the reasons are: safety requirements, insurance rates, interface with fire department personnel, knowledge of alarm panels, fire fighting equipment, sprinklers, and emergency procedures.

Education in the area of Fire Science is often thought to be needed only by those people in the area of fire suppression. With today's overlapping of professions and responsibilities, as well as needed cooperation among different agencies, this is no longer the case.

When we think of fire science we often picture learning how to operate apparatus and fight fires. Though this is part of fire science, it is just a small percentage of what the subject truly entails. The area of fire protection has developed far beyond that. As the world progresses so must fire protection. Today we have a fast changing life style and with that the problems of fire protection have grown. Thus responsibility for fire protection has grown beyond the range of fire suppression personnel. Today it takes a joint effort by many people inside and outside (police security personnel) the fire service. This is why education in fire science has to go beyond fire suppression agencies.

Three fields which can find benefit from fire science education are security/loss prevention, law enforcement, and safety. Though fire protection may seem quite distant to these professions, there are many connecting factors.

Fire Science Education

The individual entering security/loss prevention will often feel that knowing fire is important for fire departments only. At face value this could appear to be true, but fire departments must often depend on loss prevention personnel as a primary support group. All levels of security/loss prevention personnel may come in contact and have to coordinate with fire personnel.

Learning what fire departments do and how they operate will make for better coordination between the fire service and security management. A joint effort is always more successful than two independent operations. The better the two understand each other, the better coordination will be. For loss prevention personnel at the scene of a fire, self-preservation could be a major reason for fire science education. Although fire units will be in route to the scene in moments with a full compliment of equipment, protective gear, and training, it is not uncommon to have loss prevention personnel on the premises at a fire scene or emergency. It is a natural instinct to try to do something proactive to protect life and property. Those few seconds when we are alone and feel that impulse to do something, could be hazardous. If we do not know the characteristics of a fire or how it progresses, what it takes to extinguish it in its different stages, its life threatening features, and the speed at which it develops, we may not only not stop the fire, but may complicate fire fighting operations by becoming another victim. We cannot deal with or combat something we know little or nothing about. One must know when to act and when to retreat.

In addition many other aspects of security employment may require education in fire science. First, and obviously, their initial employment may require it. Many companies have consolidated the functions of loss prevention and fire control to save on hiring two individuals. Loss prevention personnel are going to be on the premises around the clock so there is a feeling that since they are present they may as well handle both functions.

Alarm panels located in a central observation area may be accompanied by fire detection panels. A person could watch two panels as well as one. When a fire panel is present one must understand how to interpret what it is signaling and know how to transmit that information to the appropriate agencies. Panels may show a trouble circuit as well as an alarm circuit. Without an understanding of alarm panels, one may not know that trouble circuits show that the system is malfunctioning due to a broken wire, bad detector, etc. Knowing that a light comes on does not mean you understand what it is trying to indicate. Once the alarm sounds, how do we transmit it to the local emergency service agencies? What specific information can we give them? What questions could they ask us that we should be able to answer? Do we have a plan on the premises that we are to follow coordinating with outside agencies? When the alarm light flashes, our work could just be beginning!

Preplanning

Loss prevention personnel have a benefit which few other people do -- to control one's future. Fire departments offer a service known as pre-planning. Preplanning consists of playing the game of "what if?" The better we understand fire departments and how they operate in a fire suppression or rescue mode, the better we can coordinate our resources with their operations to meet the same end, reduce or prevent loss.

We can study our buildings and complex with the local fire department and develop a game plan should an emergency occur. This allows us to zero in on the specifics of our building and streamline operations to fit our needs. Areas of consideration could include evacuation, fire suppression features of the structure, fire apparatus and placement as well as use of emergency service personnel. While controlling a complex for non-approved entry, we must still have contingent plans should access or evacuation be necessary on a major scale. For example, in a large factory we may have personnel monitoring the premises or physically making rounds to check the security of the complex. During evenings, weekends, or slack time there may be a minimal number of personnel on the grounds. Should an emergency occur, preparing to coordinate responding emergency units could be hectic. Access to the plant is necessary if gates and security barriers are in place. Who is going to physically open them? If we are dealing with a large complex, who is going to direct emergency units to specific buildings, warehouses, or wings? Maintenance or fire brigade personnel may be on the scene and with a predetermined plan, they may have some operations. What has been done, and what has yet to be done? What specific information can we give fire department personnel as to the nature of the problem, who is involved, and what is or is not presently being done to remedy it?

When fire apparatus arrives on the scene it needs more than a place to park. Where is the best place to position a vehicle? Could it be too close or too far away from the building? Do we have water hydrants located at key locations for easy connection? If we are not attune to how fire apparatus functions, we could put them in a losing position. Water must be available in large quantities at a reasonable distance for fire apparatus. Key positions are needed in front, behind, and even possibly on the sides of buildings to control and extinguish given fires. Unconsciously we can work against these ideas by not keeping access lanes open to structures. Employee parking, exterior stock, or production equipment may cause the perimeter of the area to be congested. When we know, talk, and plan with emergency personnel, we can deal with these problems.

If a building is equipped with fire suppression equipment such as sprinkler systems, standpipe systems, or even fire extinguishers, what do loss prevention personnel need to know? The sprinkler system could and may be connected to our alarm system. Can we distinguish sprinkler alarms and fire alarms from pull stations? If we do have a sprinkler system there should be an outside connection to which fire apparatus could connect to increase pressure on the system should it be necessary. Do we know where it is, is there access to it, is there access to the nearest water hydrant, has maintenance kept that sprinkler connection in an operational condition? It is too late to check all this when the alarm comes in. Obviously with the activation of a sprinkler system there is going to be water flowing somewhere in the building. The need for a planned salvage operation is important. What the fire has not destroyed, the water may. Have we learned how to elevate stock to keep it off the floor or storage racks away from walls to prevent run on? What do we have on the premises to protect exposed stock and speed up the clean up operations? What plans and resources does the fire department have that can benefit our salvage operations? And finally, what employees do we have or contact to help with the salvage operation and put the sprinkler system back into operation?

Should there be a standpipe system on the premises, there may be a desire to have fire security personnel work together in a joint operation. This could lead to the development of an on premises fire brigade. First, it must be decided if any fire fighting is going to be done by the employees. If not, plans should be made and developed for an evacuation and getting outside help as soon as possible. If fire fighting is going to be done, we must decide to what level it will be done. With a standpipe system we must know how to operate it and its limitations. If interior firefighting is going to be done, training, equipment, and personal protection gear is going to be needed. A fire of size is one which is beyond the capabilities of the layman with a fire extinguisher. It takes more planning, preparation, and commitment by management as well as the people directly involved. Should the simplest of levels be desired, that of fighting just incipient stage fire with fire extinguishers, then that training should be given so that security personnel are proficient and contingent plans should be made in case the situation develops beyond control of extinguishers.

Hazardous Materials

Today there is a great concern about hazardous materials. In the past we have had a tendency to consider them as something which is only found in high hazard production situations. To the contrary, we can find hazardous materials in places ranging from our home to almost any place people could occupy. It should be understood that hazardous materials can be found in storage, production, and in finished products. Areas where there is truck, rail, or any type of delivery access, can always be subject to a hazardous material incident. Trucks or trains which make deliveries or pick-ups may carry hazardous items unknown to us. Should an accident or derailment occur we may be dealing with a product of unknown composition. Do trucks of a certain design indicate certain types of loads, what features do those trucks have to control or stop leaks, where can we find shipping papers or labeling to indicate what is being carried? Who on rail cars can tell us what is in each car and where can we find papers describing content? Who do we contact on a local, state, or federal level for assistance and to report the situation to the proper authorities? All of this must be done and done quickly with no confusion. In cases like this we are dealing with a situation which can move and kill faster than a fire. Small amounts of chemicals can expand to great volumes once in the atmosphere. Should evacuation need to go beyond the immediate area, it may be necessary to extend the damage zone to public areas. Good relations and planning with public emergency services can get this accomplished quicker.

In contrast to manufacturing and distribution, we must consider places where the public is at risk. Today, we have large complexes for shopping and entertainment. Though the fire load may appear to be less than that of a manufacturing plant, in reality it may be greater. All those petroleum base materials which were in storage or processing are now stored as automobile tires, home furnishings, building material, and even dressing apparel. The difference now is that in addition to a warehouse full of combustibles, we have a mall or shopping center filled with people. Large shopping centers can sprall over a large area. From the doors where one walks in to the shop on the end could be great distance. Fire apparatus placed in front of a mall could be a great distance away from a fire. When we look at exiting we realize that most of the doors in a mall take us into shops or out of them. We may not stay attuned to those which lead us to the outside. The entrance where we came in from our car may be the only one with which we are familiar. Controlling and moving large numbers of people is always a problem.

Determining alarms and response actions in a large shopping center can be as involved as a large industrial complex. What is our panel telling us, what is our planned action, what are our resources? Loss prevention personnel in public places may unknowingly find themselves in a worse situation than others.

Arson

Fire can be a crime in itself or be part of one. In the loss prevention field, we can see areas where knowing the difference between an accidental fire and an incendiary fire is of major importance. Fire has been used in many ways. A disgruntled employee who has been fired, demoted, or passed over for promotion, may use it as an instrument of revenge. Theft can be hidden by a fire. It would be easy to remove stock and set a fire. Without taking a good inventory of the loss or a good look at how or why the fire started, we could overlook the reality of the incident. Some employees may find fire setting a benefit with ideas of rewards or promotions by extinguishing or reporting fires they have set themselves. Through fire education we can learn how fires start naturally and by accident. Natural and accidental fires have a definite pattern and character of their very own no matter what the fuel or ignition source. If a fire is started naturally or by accident, the elements of fuel and an ignition source will still be present even in the ashes. Burn patterns will show if a fire burned as it should or if it had help. But without knowing what to look for and how to interpret findings, we will often write off intentionally set fires as accidental.

There is a need to know how to handle an arson case and to preserve evidence. Many times good cases can be jeopardized by the inability of personnel to know when they are looking at real evidence and how to preserve it. The need to know how to coordinate with fire personnel and law enforcement agencies in developing a good case is of major importance. Loss prevention personnel with education in this area can be a pivotal point in securing the needed assistance outside agencies will need in this matter.

Inspectors

Whenever building or fire inspectors arrive on any premises they seem to bring confusion. Codes and laws relative to fire protection can be foreign to someone who does not understand them. Loss prevention personnel can benefit by understanding how fire codes and laws can affect their operation.

When original construction or renovation is done, inspectors will be present to see that safety features are included in the construction. If one does not understand what is being done or why, the integrity of the building from the point of view of loss prevention could be damaged. Points relative to fire safety can be worked out to keep a building secure as well as have the level of safety needed. But one must know what codes are being used, how they are put into use, and what the process is to maintain those levels of safety. Exiting to evacuate the public is possible without jeopardizing security. Safety systems can be implemented with protection from vandalism. But you have to know what the code says to discuss these matters.

It is not uncommon, even for fire inspectors, to have to refer to code manuals to look up different aspects of the laws. In fact, it is better to take the time to look up a particular section of the code than to give an opinion and then be wrong. When codes are involved we could be dealing with matters of a great financial investment as well as something structural which is not easy to rectify. A good inspector will not mind being asked to show where the code requires certain safety features, and a person which is affected by the code should not be afraid to ask questions. Loss prevention personnel must know the material they are discussing or else they will be at a loss.

Insurance Regulations

Insurance carriers, should they be industrial or commercial, will require certain basic standards. Should loss prevention personnel fall into a dual role of security and safety they may find themselves looking at functions they have no idea how to perform or why they need to be performed. Earlier the point of sprinkler systems and standpipe systems was discussed. These systems have to be connected to some source to supply the needed water they could require. Insurance carriers may require records showing water hydrant maintenance, flow records, suppression capabilities. Knowing that there is a water hydrant on most corners is not enough. How does one use a pitot gauge to know how much water a hydrant can deliver? If a hydrant is supposed to deliver water, why do they make dry ones? Do you turn it a little for a little water and all the way for a lot? We can take a common thing like a water hydrant and feel quite ridiculous when being asked a simple question about them, but carriers will require basic knowledge of loss prevention personnel with those responsibilities.

Access to hydrants and suppression systems must be maintained so fire apparatus can utilize them. Traffic, from auto to rail, may have to be interrupted to allow fire units to function for extended periods of time. Do you have alternate routes planned for major tie-ups in highly congested areas? Should rail lines need to stop trains, how does one contact a moving train to tell it to stop? One hose laying across a street or a set of railroad tracks which is damaged by traffic can have a far reaching effect on fire fighting capabilities.

People Control

Crowd and victim control is always a major concern to fire personnel. Once people have been taken from fire structures someone must be responsible for them. This is most important should there still be some relatives in the fire structure. It is not uncommon for a parent to reenter a building to look for an unaccounted for child who has already been rescued but out of sight for the moment. Fire and accidents seem to be a magnet for onlookers. This not only causes congestion for emergency units and personnel, but can endanger bystanders. Debris from structural fires can include anything from hot embers to large pieces of glass. Glass falling from a high rise building and being caught in the wind can drift a great distance and cut like a surgeon's knife. Crowds must be kept a great distance back from buildings, and this is easier said than done.

Coordination

Some fire departments do not have the direct authority to write tickets or court notices. This must be done by the police department. Without some understanding of fire laws and the city ordinances affecting fire safety, it is difficult for an officer to really understand what he or she is charging someone with. It takes a certain understanding and coordination with the fire department to handle such matters. This is even more clear in the case of arson. Some people are of the theory that fire departments discover arson and law enforcement agencies investigate and prosecute it. One could see why this point of view is held since law enforcement personnel do more investigations and conduct more interviews or interrogations in a month than most fire departments will do in years. It would be sad to lose a case because fire personnel did not know how to properly and legally handle a case. If law enforcement personnel are going to deal with arson, then they must have some fire education. How could someone investigate something that they know nothing about? What questions do you ask? What do you took for? Again, an education in fire science is needed for this.

Due to financial or manpower reasons, some cities may find themselves using a consolidation safety officer system. Instead of having a separate law enforcement and fire protection force, they may join them into one group. Some cities have found this to work if the idea is handled and developed correctly. It is obvious that if this system were considered, education in fire protection would have to be extensive. Some education in fire science could be a good base to build from. It takes time, training, and hands-on development to become a firefighter. No one class is going to do it all. But each will be a good building block to develop a strong background.

Safety is an area which can be combined with other responsibilities. This could include everything from loss prevention to maintenance. There may be requirements by insurance carriers as well as governmental agencies to have safety programs on the premises. Again, without some prior knowledge, one could be lost in a vast unknown area.

One constant that has been continually brought up in this paper is still a primary motivator for fire education the need for coordination. Whether small or large scale, agencies must coordinate. Should large catastrophes strike such as tornadoes, earthquakes, or hazardous material incidents, all agencies at all levels will be working together. Whole city blocks will be the focus of emergency agencies and law enforcement personnel. No one will succeed alone without the help of other departments and agencies ranging from the local to the state level. We need to know what each other's needs are so we can direct our resources toward a common end.

Exit and emergency routes for employees may have to be prepared, posted, and explained. Should partial or total evacuations be required, one must know who is to stay and who is to go. Certain systems in the building may require key operating personnel to stay on line to control operational functions which could make the situation worse. For example in a nuclear power plant, operators may not be able to leave immediately and ignore the system. Alternate evacuation plans will have to be tailored for their needs.

When there are large building complexes with employees or customers in them, there is always the possibility of heart attack, injury, or an industrial accident. Planning and preparation is a prime ingredient in these matters. In a large shopping mall, communications, access for emergency services, and long distances to cover must be considered. In industry there is the threat of an accident with almost any operation where there is mechanical equipment in operation. In a commercial setting no better customer relations can be found than by helping someone in medical need. Good safety programs in industry can hopefully make for better employee awareness towards safety and possibly reduction in employee leave time due to preventable injuries.

Safety programs could include basic training with an understanding of portable fire extinguishers. Though not as advanced as some levels of loss prevention, this could solve a fire problem in its early stages. Employee awareness of extinguisher locations, their fire fighting capabilities, and their use is a good investment in any company.

Conclusions

We have discussed many aspects supporting the need for fire education in the areas of loss prevention, law enforcement, and safety. If we look at the facts we will see that areas ranging from our homes to our jobs, the threat of fire loss exists everywhere. Our losses may be physical or financial at almost any level. It is no longer a world where any one person, company, or agency can stand on their own with the odds of loss being what they are. Education in and preparation for fire can be an investment which could provide substantial returns for ourselves, our companies, and the general public at large.

CHAPTER 11

DISASTER PLANNING CONSIDERATIONS FOR THE SECURITY / SAFETY PROFESSIONAL: A HISTORICAL INTERFACE

Dennis F. Sigwart, Ph.D., Professor
Western Illinois University, Health Sciences

Prevention of loss includes negating the opportunity for accidents, and disasters of ever occurring. Second, if they·do occur, then part of ones plan should be how to minimize the damages. In addition, the recovery effort must be included in any disaster plan.

OVERVIEW

Current and future security professionals should be aware of the absolute essentiality of disaster planning and preparedness as a viable component of the many facets of which they will have to perform as a practitioner. Those assigned disaster preparedness tasks must continually play the "what happens if game." While not all eventualities can be planned for (Murphy's Law can come forward at any time), to neglect planning totally, or to give mere lip-service to it, is indeed foolhardy.

Having a plan is critical to emergency and disaster planning. In general a plan for each type of emergency or disaster should be in place. The plans should address the issues of continuity of management, protection of vital records, control centers, types of emergencies, goals of emergency efforts, testing and drills for preparedness, utilization of a "mutual aid" agreement (call up list of local resources that would be contacted to help), evacuation procedures, emergency shutdown, and restoration or recovery procedures (*Protection of Assets Manual*, Merritt Company, 1984).

With such plans the recovery process will be less difficult. Courses which might be beneficial would be fire/safety loss prevention, emergency management, disaster procedures, hazardous materials, insurance, seminars and certain management courses.

The following article offers some basic thoughts and ideas to serve as a framework and foundation for those embarking on a career that includes some responsibility for disaster survivability.

Humans have been plagued throughout history by various types of disasters and catastrophes. A disaster may be defined in a number of ways, with a common operational definition that it is a major emergency affecting a large number of people. It is an occurrence that can result in loss of life, serious injury, and property damage.

Disasters may be classified as natural or human-made. The natural disaster is caused by environmental conditions, such as severe weather, volcanoes, or earthquakes. The human-made variety is one produced by people, usually in a human-error activity in combination with technological malfunctions (Bever 1988); 166-71). Examples of this type of disaster are the Titanic sinking, the Challenger explosion, the Hindenburg crash, and the Bhopal, India calamity.

Although the United States has not suffered from disasters to the same extent as other countries, in each year of this century in excess of one thousand people have perished in disasters. These tragedies often receive priority news coverage, have dramatic impact, and often result in safety measure implementations and/or countermeasures to prevent reoccurrence (See Chart 1). However, the annual loss of life from disasters is small when compared to the total number of deaths from all types of accidents (i.e., the casualties in aviation annually versus the cumulative loss of life in all accidents).

CHART 1

DISASTERS, CASUALTIES, AND RESULTING ACTIONS

DISASTER	DATE	DEATHS	RESULT
Titanic	4-15-12	1517	Lifeboat Regulations
New London Texas School Explosion	3-18-37	294	Odorants in Natural Gas
Monongah West Virginia Coal Mine Explosion	12-6-07	361	Created Federal Bureau of Mines
Two Plane Collision Over Grand Canyon	6-30-56	128	Widen Air Spaces

Enterprises can offset the impact of disaster by planned and organized action that is commonly referred to as disaster preparedness. Some elementary objectives of disaster preparedness include, but are not limited to, the protection of lives and property, the preservation of organizational structure of the organization/institution, and the assurance of the resumption of production or services (West Virginia University 1971; 14). To be considered functional, the plan must be able to reduce death, disability, and property loss; be able to limit the emotional impact of the disaster; be capable of publicizing the nature of the threat; and enable participation in planning and practice drills by the served clientele.

If planning is to be an integral part of a disaster survivable then certain planning elements, used as guidance tools, should be considered in order to develop such an overall design. These could include, but not be confined to, the following sequential steps:

Assess vulnerability of the area for which the plan is being made. For example, a disaster plan in the midwest would assess the threat of tornadoes and winter storms but not be overly concerned with hurricanes. A chemical plant would seriously consider the consequences of fire and explosion but not be particularly worried about the spread of nosocomial disease (hospital acquired disease).

In short, the plan should reflect the most likely trauma-producing incidences.

Take inventory of available community resources (police, fire department, service group support, national guard capabilities, hospital services, etc.) in order to determine if, in fact, it is feasible to combat the threats pinpointed in the assessment stage.

Develop the plan with various community or enterprise group representatives. This will likely involve extensive meeting time on the part of the plan developers since there are no "quick fixes" to disaster planning -- only hard work.

Coordinate the various preparedness plans that have been derived in the development phase. This will involve the same people that participated in the conception of the plan and their immediate subordinates (fire chief, deputy fire chief, operations officer, etc.) taking the necessary actions to make the plan something more than a paper document.

Once the disaster preparedness plan is written and put into a workable format, it must be integrated into the daily life of the community or into the group that it is designed to protect. The people affected by the plan must be informed as to its details and to what is expected of them as individuals and as leaders in the eventuality of a disaster.

Practice drills are a MUST in order to "work out the bugs" of the plan. Such activities as these can give indications as to the reliability of the document and its workability. It is never too early in the "game" to find out if the plan is viable.

With the completion of the practice drill(s), an evaluation can be completed, changes made, and reinforcement of those positive things brought to the forefront (West Virginia University 1971; 4).

While the loss of material goods and property damage are of paramount importance in any disaster, the human problems as a result of an impacting calamity may have to be dealt with the highest priority. Water, food, shelter, emergency care, and personal protection are but a few of the issues that will confront a community or organization in an emergency, and a plan must deal with these issues. Chart 2 lists the typical human problems as a result of disaster and suggested agencies that could render assistance for that particular dilemma relative to the loss-bearing incident.

CHART 2

TYPICAL HUMAN PROBLEMS AS A RESULT OF DISASTER AND POTENTIAL AGENCIES FOR ASSISTANCE

Shelter	Civil Defense and Red Cross
Food	Red Cross and Civic Groups
Water	Civil Government
Emergency Care	Hospitals and Clinics
Medical Evaluations	Hospitals and Health Agencies
Personal Protection	Police and National Guard
Illumination	Public Utilities
Communications	Citizen Ban Radio and National Guard
Transportation	National Guard, Local Trucking, and Bus Companies
Property Protection	Police, Auxiliary Police, and National Guard

In order to expedite planning for disasters, some knowledge of the concept of the principle elements common to most disasters -- time coordinates and space coordinates -- may be of benefit for the would-be planner. Chart 3 and Chart 4 depict the time coordinate and the space coordinate respectively.

CHART 3

TIME COORDINATE OF DISASTERS

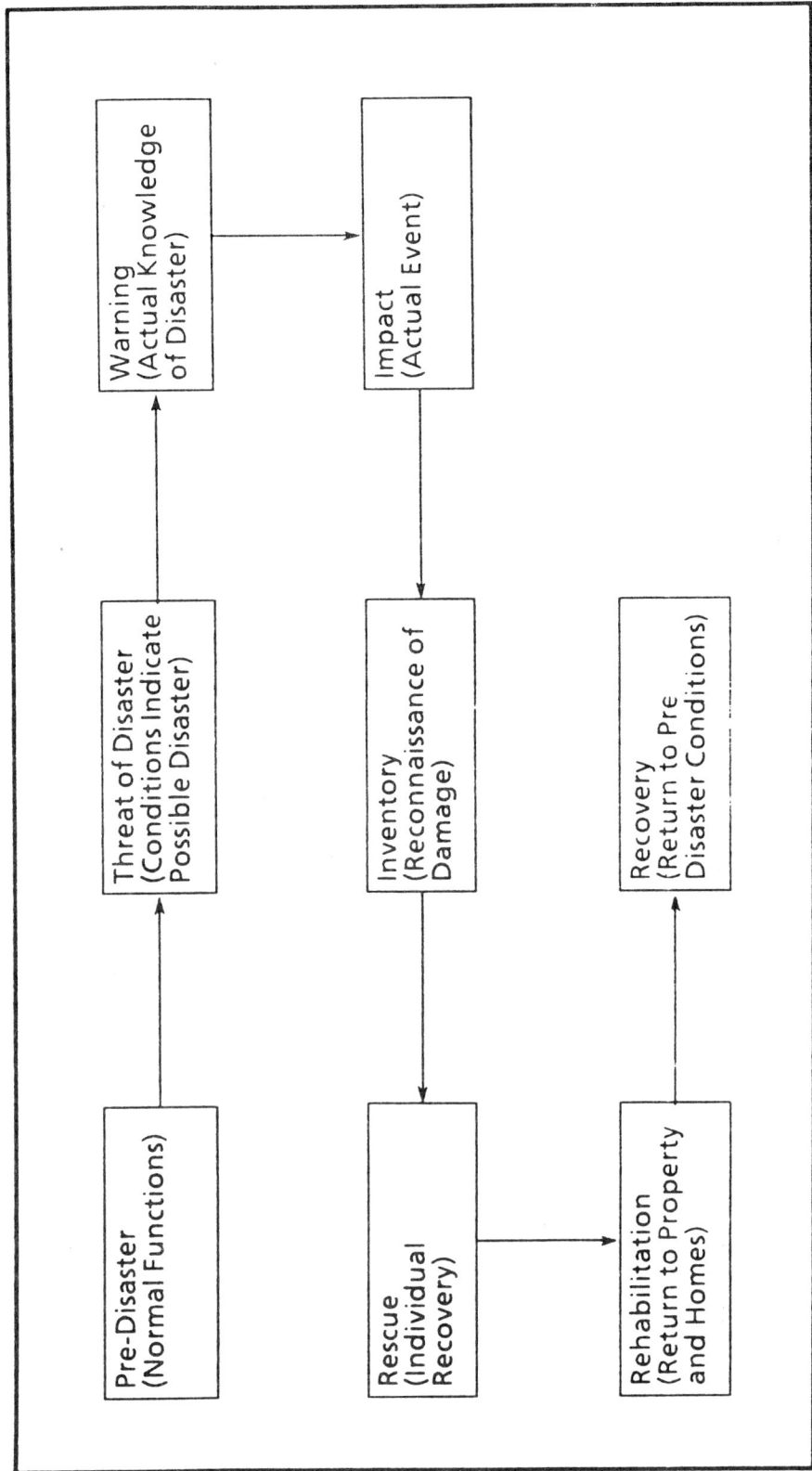

CHART 4

SPACE COORDINATE OF DISASTERS

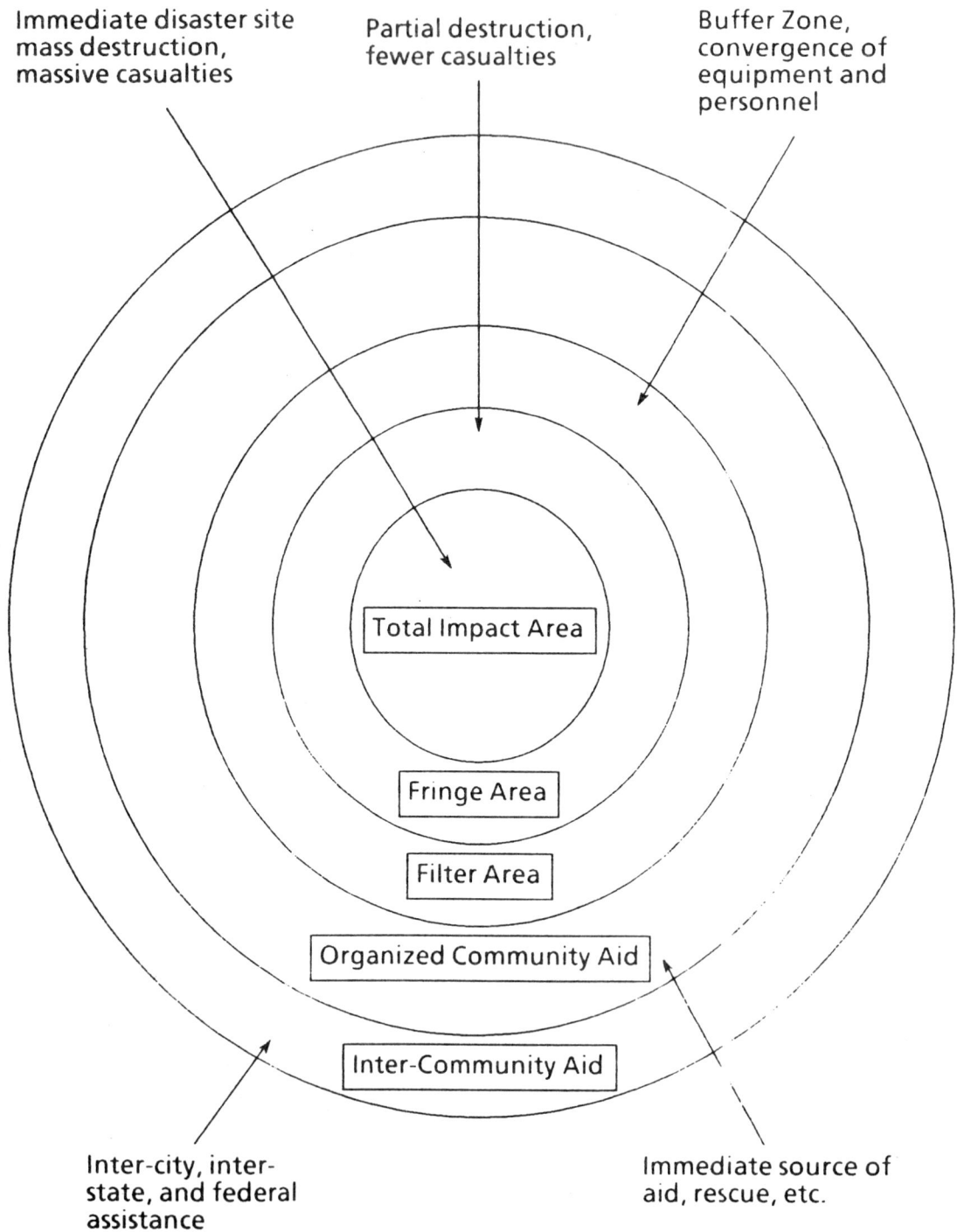

Immediate disaster site mass destruction, massive casualties

Partial destruction, fewer casualties

Buffer Zone, convergence of equipment and personnel

Total Impact Area

Fringe Area

Filter Area

Organized Community Aid

Inter-Community Aid

Inter-city, inter-state, and federal assistance

Immediate source of aid, rescue, etc.

The time coordinate is a specific time span that ranges from a pre-disaster phase to a recovery phase (West Virginia University 1971; 5). A brief explanation of each part follows:

PRE DISASTER: Normal functions of the individual and the community are taking place; hopefully, some disaster plans are operationally ready.

THREAT: Conditions indicate that a possible disaster may occur. Weather watches and other forms of alert are issued. This is the first indication that the disaster plan may have to be put into effect.

WARNING: The actual knowledge of an impending and imminent disaster is gained. Sighting of tornadoes, discovery of fires, and observation of chemical spills are examples of this phase of the time coordinate.

IMPACT: The actual occurrence of the disaster.

INVENTORY: A time period immediately following the impact phase in which a reconnaissance of the damage is conducted and casualties assessed.

RESCUE: Activities such as emergency care and rescue operations are carried out.

REHABILITATION: People return to their property and work environments.

RECOVERY: A return to pre-disaster conditions.

The space coordinates relate to geographic positioning relative to the impact of disaster (New York Times, 1911). The elements of this concept are as follows:

TOTAL IMPACT AREA: This is the immediate disaster site containing the majority of the dead, injured, and property loss/damage

FRINGE AREA: An area characterized by partial destruction, and fewer casualties than the total impact areas, but nevertheless a location of trauma, confusion, and tension.

FILTER AREA: A buffer zone between the remaining unaffected community and the disaster site.

ORGANIZED COMMUNITY AID: The immediate source of material, services, and aid will come from the component of the coordinate. For example, the fire department will respond from this area as well as utility company emergency teams.

INTER COMMUNITY AID: Inter-city, interstate, and federal aid are potential sources of assistance in recovery operations. Federal money for the reconstruction of communication capabilities within a municipality may be an example of this concept.

The following case study of the Triangle Shirtwaist factory fire of 1911 will serve as a illustration of the previously described time and space coordinates. Interjected within this portrayal will be brackets and parentheses offsetting the particular time or space coordinate. the give element will be segregated in brackets, and within these parentheses will designate the time or space coordinates. For example, [IMPACT (SPACE)] means that the impact phase of the space coordinate is taking place in the flow of events. Likewise, [WARNING (TIME)] is read as the warning facet of the time coordinate.

One of the most rampaging and life-destroying fires in United States history was the Triangle Shirtwaist factory fire of March 25, 1911. In its wake, this New York City blaze left one hundred forty six employees dead in a mere eighteen minutes. Most of the victims were young women who either burned to death, died of smoke inhalation, or were forced to jump to their deaths onto the streets and sidewalks adjacent to the building.

The fire was confined to three stories, the eighth, ninth, and tenth [IMPACT (SPACE)], but it was the most murderous fire in New York City since the burning of the excursion boat the "General Slocum." The building was supposedly fire-proof and investigations the following day supported this contention. The walls and floors showed little if any destruction; only the stock and the victims suffered the consequences of the inferno. However, there were design defects relative to fire safety in the structure [THREAT (TIME)]. For instance, there were no automatic sprinklers for extinguishment, and there was only one street-to-roof stairwell. A second stairway extended solely to the tenth floor and at the back of the building, a fire escape descended to the second floor, thus creating a predicament whereby anyone desiring escape by this mode would be forced to jump the remaining two stories onto concrete [THREAT (TIME)]. Finally, the owners of the company, as a theft-prevention countermeasure, installed narrow exists to allow for the inspection of personnel upon leaving the confines of the work area at quitting time ['THREAT (TIME)]. It is probable that this restriction to egress resulted in numerous lives being lost (New York Times, 1911).

When the fire broke out at 4:45 p.m. [IMPACT (TIME)], almost quitting time for the day, those present felt it could be contained. But the fire "flashed" and spread rapidly through a fabric remnants bin on the eighth floor, and when management tried to apply water from hoses, no pressure was available. Thus, the flames deployed quickly, engulfing the entire area [IMPACT (TIME), IMPACT AND FRINGE (SPACE)] and a panic followed.

No warning had been given [WARNING (TIME)] on the ninth floor [IMPACT (SPACE)] and when the flames erupted, the workers ran for the single exit available only to discover it was locked. Many of these people then were forced to jump from windows. Meanwhile, a warning had been given to the tenth floor [IMPACT (SPACE)] via telephone, and as a consequence, people either joined in the rush down the crowded stairs or climbed to the roof (FILTER (SPACE)]. Some of the terror-infested employees threw themselves on a descending elevator roof only to be killed by the bodies of those who fell or jumped on top of them.

By the time the first firefighting unit arrived [ORGANIZED COMMUNITY AID (SPACE)], the fire was beyond control. People were Jumping from the building, and firemen soon found that their ladders could only reach to the sixth floor [FILTER (SPACE)], and their water hoses could not stretch to the trapped victims on the window ledges.

The firefighters' nets proved to be ineffective as the jumpers' bodies tore through the canvas, bringing instant death. Eventually, the fire hoses became so covered with the dead that the mutual weight of the corpses hindered the water flow [FILTER (SPACE)]. As mentioned previously, all of the fatalities, destruction, and sorrow occurred in eighteen minutes IPRE DISASTER THROUGH RESCUE (TIME)].

Although one hundred forty six victims paid the ultimate price for the disaster, some benefits came from the tragedy. In general. the conflagration brought about stricter safety regulations and more quality fire fighting devices [RECOVER (TIME)]. However, these advancements would not be apparent for years. Another direct result of the fire was the strengthening of the International Ladies Garment Workers Union, which in turn played a strong advocacy role in bringing about needed changes [RECOVERY (TIME)] (New York Times, 1911).

Lessons learned from this fire are easily concluded if not original. As is the case in many disasters, the game of speculation of "what if" could be played. Obviously, automatic sprinklers would have altered the outcome significantly. Further, adequate fire drills and egress instructions to the work force as well as training in proper conduct during a fire could have reaped benefits in terms of lives saved.

If sufficient exits had been present, many people could have escaped, and if proper storage of flammable fabric and combustible materials had been practiced, the outcome of that grisly afternoon could have possibly been different. Since none of the above was in fact a reality on March, 25, 1911, history has recorded this as a grim day in the annals of fire loss in the United States.

In summary, while disasters are unpredictable, they can be combated. Knowledge and warning are two principle means of offsetting the catastrophic affects of disasters, but the foresight to plan and implement emergency countermeasures are paramount to success for survival and damage limitations. As discussed in this article, considerations for devising a disaster preparedness plan could include, but not be limited to, the following: a review of planning elements; cognizance of typical human problems as a result of disasters; a regard for particular elements common to disaster, and some comprehension/knowledge of historical case studies, or history in general, to serve as a basis for future mitigation efforts. All of these could be beneficial in plan development.

"Prior proper planning prevents poor performance" is in old adage that certainly pertains to the business of disaster preparedness and should be kept in mind by security and safety practitioners and professionals when they become involved in disaster countermeasure activities.

References

Anton, Thomas J. 1989. <u>Occupational Safety and Health Management</u>. New York: McGraw-Hill Co.

Bever, David L. 1988. <u>Safety: A Personal Focus</u>. St Louis: Times Mirror/Mosby Co.

Hammer, Willie. 1976. <u>Occupational Safety Management and Engineering</u>. Englewood Cliffs, New Jersey: Prentice-Hall Inc

<u>New York Times</u>. 1911. "Triangle Shirtwaste Factory Fire," March 26.

Walsh Timothy J., CPP and Richard J. Healy, CPP. 1984. <u>Protection of Assets Manual</u>, Merritt Company.

West Virginia University. 1971. <u>Safety Studies 233 Disaster Preparedness and Emergency Systems Course Outline</u>. Morgantown, West Virginia.

Worick, Wayne. 1975. <u>Safety Education</u>. Englewood Cliffs, New Jersey: Prentice-Hall.

CHAPTER 12

RISK MANAGEMENT AND INSURANCE: TOOLS FOR SECURITY PROFESSIONALS

Joseph A. Panici, Associate Professor of Insurance
Western Illinois University

Discussion of risk management's role in attempting to determine exposure to risk (how much risk there is, how great is the risk, how much insurance and countermeasures are needed). The idea is not only to protect ones assets but to eliminate the risk if possible. The importance of studying in this area is explained.

As the insurance professor at a Midwestern university for the past twenty years, I have noticed the following question surfacing on numerous occasions. "If I am a student in the college of Law Enforcement and Justice Administration (LEJA) and majoring in security, "Why should I have to learn about insurance or risk management? After all, those are business courses, aren't they?" LEJA students with majors in security are required to take my insurance course, and it is these students who ask the above question. They surely ask it silently to themselves, sometimes they ask their LEJA professors or advisors, and occasionally they have asked me.

At first the answer was not quite as clear to me as it is now. Perhaps this was due to my preconceived and outdated notion that security personnel were generally elderly men with uniforms, a gun, a flashlight, and perhaps a CCTV monitor to stare at while drinking coffee and trying to stay awake. Once I investigated the "other college" (LEJA) within my university and its security course and program, it became apparent to me that our two areas really do have much more in common than initially comes to mind. In fact, one could say that a marriage of sorts exists between the risk manager and the security manager of a particular business because of a common goal. Please allow me to explain.

Suppose the following question was asked of two separate classes here on campus. One is a "security management" class and the other is across campus in the college of business and is in "principles of insurance." The question posed to both classes is as follows: From the following job description you are to identify the person by job title, whose responsibilities within the corporation are as follows. Fill in the blank.

The primary and fundamental objective of the _____ manager is the preservation of assets and earning power from loss or destruction. He or she shall be responsible for identifying all exposures to such loss. The financial risk associated with each such exposure to loss must be evaluated as to both its severity and probability of occurrence. An action must then be taken to either eliminate said risks or reduce either the probability of their occurrence or the severity of their consequences. In summation, he/she is charged with preserving the operating effectiveness of the corporation by safeguarding both its assets and its potential income.

How to you suppose our two groups would answer this question? You can rest assured that the security class thought that the job description was right out of their security textbook, and was in fact describing the duties of the head of security or security manager. They would have filled in the blank with the word security. The business students on the other hand would have recognized that the description of duties fit the risk manager to a tee. The insurance class would therefore have filled in the blank with the word risk. Now that is interesting! Risk and security are opposites of one another and yet those words would have shown up as the students' answers to the same question. Why? Well, one reason is that security is the counterpart of risk. The effective treatment of risks yields security. The two disciplines are as similar as two peas in a pod.

This notion of sameness of goal or purpose was apparent to me the first time I perused a textbook on security. It was *deja'vu*; I had been through all this before. Even though I had never before read a textbook on security, the content was quite familiar to me. In fact, with the exception of a few chapters, the title to much of the text could well have been changed to risk management. For example, consider the following:

A popular security text, which is used at this university, notes that security "... implies a stable, relatively predictable environment in which an individual or group may pursue its ends without disruption or harm, and without fear of such disturbance or injury." That same text indicates that private security includes all protective and loss-prevention activities not performed by law enforcement agencies. This textbook even includes one chapter on insurance and another on risk management. I can understand why the security class would have answered my hypothetical exam question the way they did.

Without wanting to give a complete treatise on risk management, its definition's similarity to those listed above should be pointed out. Turning our attention to my insurance/risk management texts will show why the insurance students answered the hypothetical question as they did. Risk management has been variously described as... "managing major classes of exposure to loss;" "the process of conserving the earning power and assets by minimizing the financial effects of accidental loss;" and ... "dealing with pure risks faced by individuals and businesses." The risk manager's consummate goal then is to assure that same, stable economic environment that the director of security is also striving for. Every business firm faces the risks associated with potential destruction or loss of plant and equipment from the perils of fire, flood, lightning, theft, tornado, etc. Risk is the potential for economic loss flowing from these and a myriad of other perils. If we can somehow eliminate or reduce the possibility of loss from the perils of fire, embezzlement, or any other peril, then we have preserved an asset and prevented the firm from suffering an economic loss. To achieve this goal is the common link between the chief or head of security and the risk manager. To be sure, they have many overlapping objectives to attain.

The aforementioned objectives and goals of the two separate departmental managers are interwoven in such a manner as to strongly suggest, if not mandate, that the two managers must work together cooperatively. In smaller businesses, there may be some combination of these two positions. Very small businesses may actually employ one individual to do it all. However, in large firms, there may be a separate manager for non-insurable risks, another for insurable pure risks, another for loss prevention activities, and still others for bonding or other miscellaneous functions. It is within these larger firms that a cooperative effort between all management personnel is vitally necessary with information exchanged and flowing between departments. The more knowledge the security professional has about risk management and insurance, the better he or she will be equipped for such communication.

Consider for a moment the following communication breakdown and its potentially catastrophic impact on the firm. A large multi-national corporation acquired a corporate jet for its executives. Nobody bothered to tell the risk manager of the acquisition. What is so terribly wrong with that, you ask? Well, for starters, the typical corporate insurance policy excludes all liability arising out of owned aircraft! Please do not misinterpret this example. I am not suggesting that it was the security manager's duty to inform the manager, but merely citing this as an example of potential pitfalls of communication breakdown. If the risk manager had known of the acquisition, arrangements would have been made to secure a proper insurance endorsement. As it was, the company flew all over the world in a corporate jet with no liability insurance coverage for over three months.

This leads me to a very important point concerning risk management. The preceding example was not suggesting that we necessarily need to insure all risks. Most of my students have the misconception, at least initially, that since risk and insurance go together in the same course, that the risk manager's job is to insure everything. Nothing could be further from the truth. In fact, it is just the opposite. The risk manager knows that insurance is usually the most costly of the many alternatives available for treating risk. Even unsophisticated insurance consumers should realize that insurers need to collect the amount of money they expect to pay out for claims plus considerably more to cover overhead, profit, etc. With this fact in mind, the risk manager focuses first on all of the other ways of dealing with risk that are at his disposal. It is not my intent here to give a lesson in risk management, but it may be necessary to discuss some of these non-insurance risk treatment methods to further cement the bond between risk manager and head of security. A series of examples should suffice to illustrate this point.

Risk management texts normally show risk elimination as the preferred method of dealing with risk. Common sense dictates that we cannot possibly eliminate all risk faced by the firm. Some risk though, can definitely be eliminated. Whatever risk we cannot eliminate should be reduced (controlled) as much as possible. Any residual risk after our efforts to eliminate or reduce could either be avoided, retained, or lastly .... transferred. Suppose we have a retail firm that faces the risk of loss of merchandise due to shoplifting. We know the security manager cannot eliminate this risk altogether, but can perhaps reduce it. Insurance coverage is not an option, since insurers exclude this type of loss even in their crime insurance forms. Our firm also faces potential loss from employee crime. The risk manager knows that purchasing a fidelity bond will cover this potential loss but still involves the security director in helping to screen employee records. The risk manager realizes the necessity of screening since the bonding agreements exclude coverage for losses that are traceable to an employee with a past criminal record. We also face the risk of property loss due to burglary, and although insurance is purchased, we want to involve the security professional because our burglary policy contains a warranty to the effect that our policy is canceled if our required protection devices are inoperable at the time of loss. I hope the reader begins to see the importance of a good working relationship between the risk management department and other security professionals. .

So even though we consider buying insurance to be the final alternative, we still end up buying a lot of it. Why? There are some other interesting (to security professionals) reasons for buying insurance other than to safeguard our assets from economic loss. In many cases it is required by law or perhaps a third party. Most states require the following types of coverage:

- Automobile liability insurance

- Workmen's compensation insurance to cover work related injuries

- Dram shop liability is required of owners/operators of establishments licensed to sell alcoholic beverages

- Borrowers may be required to buy credit life insurance before the lender will grant the loan

- Borrowers are usually also required to insure the collateral property (the building you bought)

In addition to the aforementioned insurance examples, sometimes it is necessary to obtain a bond. These situations though, go far beyond the intent or the scope of this paper.

A final and very important reason for buying insurance coverage is to perhaps avail ourselves of the tremendous inspection service, engineering department, or rehabilitation services offered by the insurance companies or other insurance agencies. This final reason is possibly the most pertinent to the security professional. The insurance industry has its finger on the pulse of so many significant areas of business and industry loss data that would be especially interesting to a security manager that I can only begin to touch on them in this report. A few examples will go along way to illustrate this concept.

Boiler and machinery insurance coverage is a case in point. A steam boiler system, like we have installed here at Western Illinois University, not only supplies heat to the entire campus, but also generates electrical power to the majority of the university. We are not unique in this regard, as many large business firms do the same thing. Imagine the tremendous potential for destruction that is contained within a boiler system large enough to handle an entire university campus! If it ever exploded, damage and loss of life and bodily injury could be quite severe and possibly catastrophic. The majority of every dollar of premiums spent for this type of insurance coverage is used for the inspection services provided by the insurer. Some firms purchase this coverage in minimal amounts just to secure the inspection service and engineering expertise of the insurer. Elevator liability insurance is quite similar in that the inspection service accounts for the lion's share of the premium dollar. Recent developments have caused some insurers to sell just the inspection services on a fee basis without the need to purchase the insurance coverage. Apparently some insurers decided to capitalize on the expertise of their staff of inspectors and engineers to offer this service separately lest independent firms might spring up to offer this type of service if they did not.

These services can be especially important to the security personnel to help foresee any potential for loss of life or property. The engineering/inspection services are not only useful for the existing structures, but can be invaluable at the design or blueprint stage. For example..... a public school district planned to build a new high school with a ceiling tile which would have reduced the fire resistive rating of the structure. The substitution of an improved tile saved $1,200 per year in fire insurance premiums and also made a serious fire less likely. After the building was up, this change in tile would have been quite costly. Caught in the blueprint stage, the change was accomplished at no cost. Another example taken from the same risk management manual will further emphasize this point (Lenz, 1971).

A manufacturer of buffing wheels was assessed a $25 surcharge to its fire rate because a Bunsen burner was connected to a gas outlet by a rubber hose instead of copper tubing. I should explain that fire insurance rates are quoted per $100 of coverage purchased. In this case, a $25/$100 surcharge on a $100,000 policy amounts to $250 per year more in premiums. By spending $2 for copper tubing the manufacturer saved $250 per year. Another example from my own personal experience involves a friend who owned an auto dealership. On a routine walk through of my friend's garage, his insurance agent noticed that he did not have lids on the cans within which his mechanics put their oily hand towels. The agent notified the owner that if he would equip the trash receptacles with lids that he could save over $100 per year on fire insurance premiums. The irony of this example was that it did not cost him anything. He had the lids all along, but just never used them. You can be sure he started to after that!

The following delineates the manner in which one insurance agent aided his client with loss engineering. The client had a woodworking business in Ohio (Bickelhauopt, 1974; 27).

1. Added building for expansion -- recommended separate all steel building at opposite end of property. Rate was much lower than original masonry, wood-roof building.

2. Reviewed plans for additional construction between old and new buildings with rating bureau and company engineers and underwriters recommended incombustible construction, "S" masonry wall with fire doors.

3. Recommended masonry walls and light steel roof for a new boiler and incinerator room, and a separate paint and solvent storage room.

4. Oil boiler -- recommended Underwriters' approved combustion control equipment for burners and ignition systems, and ordered inspection which will meet state requirements.

5. Dust collector system -- recommended sprinkler-head and gravity loaded fusible link controlled damper in the return air duct.

6. Fuel tanks -- to be buried at approved distance from building, with properly designed vent and filling line.

7. Paint and storage room -- recommended standard rack to hold drums, proper grounding system, self-closing spigots, drain trough and safety trash cans, lighting in closed conduit with switches outside the room, and scoring of windows for explosion release.

This insurance agent was not just selling insurance, but providing a valuable service regarding security!

The importance of these examples should be apparent to the security professional. For some fixed properties the risk control often begins at the construction stage. A fire insurance rate schedule can usually be obtained from a local rating bureau or possibly an insurer, and could be used to point out possible deficiencies or unsafe conditions that can be corrected at the blueprint stage. Even for fixed properties that are already standing, tile schedule is still useful in a similar fashion for pinpointing potential problem areas. Some rating systems in use charge an extra amount for deficiencies while others start at a base rate and give discounts for certain safety or construction features. In either case the schedules can give the security professional an insight into desirable features and attributes surrounding a particular risk. We need to know which types of construction are safest, which alarm systems work best, what type of safe or vault affords the highest degree of protection, sprinkler systems, parapets, enclosed stairwells, standpipes, firewalls, etc., etc. All of these features and their contribution to safety are reflected in rate schedules. All are based on hard statistical evidence over many years of insuring exposures of all varieties. Burglary insurance rates reflect the crime rate of the geographic locale as well as the stealability of the property in question. They also reflect the use of various types of protection devices that could be used. This insurance information is quite useful to a security professional. It can guide the security team toward the most effective use of the limited dollars available for these various protective measures. The cost effectiveness of dollars spent on the protective devices/engineering versus higher insurance premiums or some other alternative.

Along with an understanding of the rating structure of the insurance industry and a familiarity with the services offered comes a need for an understanding of how insurance policies themselves operate. Imagine the surprise of the owner/operator of a convenience store that was open 24 hours per day, when after being held up at gunpoint and relieved of a few hundred in cash, he found out that his insurance policy did not cover this loss. Why not, you ask? Well, it seems that he purchased a burglary policy. Since the policy defines burglary as the taking of property by forced entry into a business that is closed to the public, he was not burglarized. The sad thing was that it was impossible for him to be burglarized since he was never closed! The man would have benefited from a knowledge of insurance.

An insurance course would be beneficial from this particular standpoint. You would gain an understanding of how to read and actually understand what is or is not covered by your insurance. Try to read and understand your insurance policy sometime without constantly consulting Black's Law Dictionary or an insurance textbook, or keeping an open phone line to your local insurance agent. The language of the policies is so specialized that even attorneys often cannot understand them without special training. I took the Insurance Law course at the University of Iowa Law School and noted that it was an elective course. Most law schools do not require a course in this area. In fact, the first day of class found the instructor randomly asking students why they elected to take this particular course. The answer was nearly unanimous. It was something to the effect that.... they had covered two semesters of contract law and were soon to be full fledged lawyers, but after trying to read their own auto policies (contracts after all could barely understand what they meant!

Taking one insurance or risk management course will not suddenly transform you into an expert. But you may be surprised to find out that once you learn even a modest amount of the vocabulary and methods of the insurance industry, you will become far more conversant with insurance professionals. Just being able to read and understand the contract could make you a better security professional. A case in point that immediately comes to mind involves a recent news item about one of the highest ranked men's tennis players in the world. I heard a news announcement on television that this particular tennis player had just secured a multi-million dollar insurance policy known as kidnap-ransom insurance. If the reader is unfamiliar with this type of coverage, it does exactly what the name implies. In the event of **a** kidnapping, the insurance company will pay the ransom demands up to the policy limit. It has become quite popular in recent years because of the increase in terrorism overseas combined with the multinational organization of many large American corporations. Of particular pertinence in this example is a clause in the policy that is referred to as the ..."if you say you have it, you don't" clause. The insurer is aware of the potential targeting of individuals by terrorists if it were known that someone had this unique coverage. To eliminate this problem they exclude coverage if the policy's existence is divulged. So the tennis player in question is excluded from coverage. Hopefully the terrorists were not watching this particular telecast since it could possibly have put him in even greater risk.

The security professional should know about provisions and exclusions in policies like these. Perhaps such knowledge would prevent the director of security for Coca-Cola, for example, from leaking a press release that ..."all upper echelons of management are now covered by a $20,000,000 kidnapransom policy." In fact, he would take precautions to keep that information as secret as the formula for their soft drink. He should also be aware of the fact that at this time, Italy and Argentina are excluded territories under most of the available policies. This tidbit of information would prompt him to encourage or demand that the top brass hold their European division's corporate meeting in Paris or London instead of Rome. Does the security director have to be an expert in insurance? Not at all, only a sufficient knowledge of insurance to be reasonably conversant with the risk manager is needed. Remember that they have to communicate with each other and work together. They are both part of the same team.

One final common interest shared by both the risk and security professional is disaster planning. Despite our best efforts to the contrary, disaster occur with amazing regularity. The Titanic could not sink. Chicago's McCormick Place could not burn. This decade was witness to one of the most tragic industrial accidents of all time when the gas leak at a Union Carbide plant in India cost over 1,000 lives. The 1980 and 90s experience alone included Exxon's gigantic oil spill in Alaska, hurricane Hugo and the California earthquake. Hugo's property damage alone is estimated to exceed $16 billion and the San Francisco Bay area earthquake claimed over eighty lives. Before one of these tragedies strikes is the time to formulate a plan to cope with these disasters. Then when the crisis arises, we need only implement the preconceived plan or perhaps choose between multiple plans that were drawn up in a non-emergency atmosphere. The professional within the firm, the police, the fire department, hospitals, and yes ... the risk manager. An effective disaster plan could substantially reduce the economic impact of the catastrophic event. Our quest is an economically "stable environment;" no surprises, just "economic security."

That brings us full circle back to our hypothetical test question. The "stable environment" and "economic security" referred to above, were parts of definitions we found in textbooks from the two different disciplines. They are, however, a part of the same overall management objective. Now when a student asks me what importance an insurance course is to a security major, how do I answer?

I have them take my American Heritage Dictionary off the shelf and look up two words: "insure" and "security."
SECURITY: freedom from risk, safety

INSURE: to make safe or secure

They usually do not need much more of an explanation than that!

References

Bickelhaupt, David L., <u>General</u> Insurance, 9th ed., Homewood, IL: Richard D.   Irwin, 1974. p. 27.

Lenz, Matthew, Jr., <u>Risk Management Manual</u>, Santa Monica, CA: Insurors Press, 1971. Chap. 3.

CHAPTER 13

ACADEMIC PROGRAMS IN SECURITY AND LOSS PREVENTION

John Chuvala, CPP, Associate Professor
Department of Law Enforcement and Justice Administration
Western Illinois University, Macomb, Illinois
Robert J. Fischer, Ph.D. Director
Illinois Law Enforcement Executive Institute

Security education has undeniably undergone tremendous growth in the last ten years. Academic programs in security, with a few exceptions, are very young. Most were established within the last ten to fifteen years. In general, most have been reasonably successful, as the demand for college educated security managers continues to grow. Leaders in the field, both academics and practitioners, indicate that security should seek recognition as its own distinct area of study. While some believe that the programs can find this autonomy within the criminal justice field, others believe that the field would be better off in colleges of business.

No matter what the view of security education and training might be, the reality is that the field is here to stay. As recent surveys indicate, more and more security managers are seeking, or already possess, degrees. In addition, training standards are being mandated by a number of states, and some companies are already recognizing the financial benefits of a trained professional staff..

What To Look For In An Academic Program

What Courses are Offered ?

In addition to the fields of study recommended in the other chapters of this book, the student should consider taking courses in internal security, external security, security management, organized crime, computer security, white collar crime, special issues, criminological theory, ethics, and industrial security to name a few. (Special issues could include risk management, executive protection, and anti-terrorism methods.)

Student Organizations

It would be prudent to join student organizations relative to the field of study (whether they are in law enforcement, corrections, or security). In the case of security or loss prevention I refer to the American Society for Industrial Security. The advantages of joining as a student are numerous. The student becomes eligible to receive the monthly magazine *Security*

Management, has access to a placement service, and the opportunity to attend conferences in order to gain valuable information and to network.

Internships

The opportunity for the student to receive some first hand experience in the field of their choice is an extremely important factor to be considered. Internships often times end up in job offers to the intern. Even if a job isn't the end result, the experience is invaluable. In addition, this offers the student the chance to see if they really want to work in police, the courts, corrections, or security.

The Value Of Security Education

Among security practitioners, security education is touted as invaluable. Among the institutions of higher learning where these courses must be offered, however, security programs continue to fight an uphill battle for survival, competing against a host of other specialties for limited university dollars, resources, and attention. Programs are often introduced only to be killed or curtailed in later years. Why does one program survive when others do not? The authors sought to answer that question with a survey of academic providers offering degrees at the baccalaureate level or above. Research conducted for *Security Management* in the early 1980s by Robert Fischer, then chairman and professor of the Law Enforcement Administration Department at Western Illinois University, identified twenty-six programs offering degrees at the baccalaureate level or above. Since that time, several attempts to keep up with the changes in security education have been made. The *Journal of Security Administration* had been publishing a list of all certificate through graduate programs until approximately 1991. In 1993, in conjunction with the Academy of Security Educators and Trainers, (ASET), Romine Deming, chairman and professor of the Department of Criminal Justice at the State University of New York, College at Brockport, compiled a listing of security programs offered in 1992. Using the Deming list with the Fischer study of 1983 and the *Journal of Security Administration* listing, our survey was conducted via a questionnaire mailed to those fifty-nine programs identified as offering degrees at the baccalaureate level or above.

An Overview

During the late 1970's and early 1980's, programs were being developed primarily by those departments offering police science and criminal justice (CJ) programs through the auspices of the Law Enforcement Assistance Administration. The American Society for Industrial Security took an interest in these developments establishing the Standing Committee on Academic Programs. Various studies, including the 1976 Task Force on Private Security, had recommended the development of programs. The task force recommended a curriculum that was 10 % sociology, 10% law enforcement/CJ, 20% security, 20% business, and 40% general education.

Kevin Parsons, of the University of Wisconsin in Oshkosh, noted in 1980 that the programs of the late 1970s were preoccupied "with locks, safes, vaults, alarms, and access control." At about the same time, Norman Bottom, Ph.D. now editor-in-chief of *Journal of Security Administration*, noted that research in private security had been minimal.

The earliest programs had several problems, as noted by Parsons. These included the following:

- Security education was dominated by police practitioners.
- Little or no concern was shown for theory in program designs.
- Little research was conducted on the effectiveness of programs.

Fischer noted that most of these programs were simply tacked onto CJ programs. By 1983, Fischer reported in the *Security Management* study that twenty-six programs offered baccalaureate or higher level degrees in security. Then, a 1985 Academy of Criminal Justice Sciences' Report revealed that more than sixty colleges (AA and above) had dropped their security degrees (most were CJ oriented). The news was reported in the June *1986 Journal of Security Administration* article, "About the Security Degree-Are We Losing It?"

Bottom noted that there was a definite conflict in basic theory between those interested in theory, or criminology; those interested in public enforcement, or criminal justice and law enforcement; and those interested in a profit-oriented approach, or private security.

Still in 1985, the *Hallcrest Report* noted that "many programs have bridged the gap between theory and practice with internship programs in business and industry." As late as 1992, Fischer noted that even though many programs had left the field, many of those remaining were doing well. Those that were doing best were well-thought-out interdisciplinary programs. Whether this judgment was true is the focus of the 1993 study.

The importance of security education is no longer debatable. ASIS, through work with Webster University, is supporting education in the security management field. Steven Langer of Langer and Associates has reported that the security manager of the 1990's is likely to be an individual with more than twenty-five years of experience, a graduate degree, and certification as a certified protection professional.

The Study

During the summer of 1993, the questionnaire used to conduct the 1981 to 1983 study for *Security Management* was updated. A total of fifty-nine programs offering baccalaureate degrees or above were identified from listings of the *Journal of Security Administration, Security Management*, and ASET. Thirty-five responses were received, providing a better-than-50 percent response rate.

Of the programs responding, most reported having established a security degree or emphasis between 1970 and 1986. The majority of those programs still offering a security program are called criminal justice degrees with a security emphasis or option. A few programs are named loss prevention, public safety, and assets protection. Fourteen programs responded by indicating that they no longer offer a degree option but are continuing to offer courses. Most of these programs are offering fewer courses than before.

The Programs

Nearly 50% of the respondents indicated that the primary motivation for establishing security programs was an impetus by individual faculty members. Another 20 percent reported that market demand, as noted by placement of graduates and inquiries from businesses, was of major importance in developing their programs. Ten percent reported that the success of programs at other institutions had been the key factor in the development of programming. The remaining 20% indicted that they were influenced by student interest, federal reports, and other reports on security education. The idea that success within a specific program can create interest in similar programs at other institutions may be important in evaluating subsequent observations and the decline of programming in many institutions.

Advisory boards had little bearing on the establishment of programs in about 50% of the responding programs. The largest, and by implication most successful, programs indicated, however, that they used and were motivated by advisory boards. Those that have used advisory boards report stable and thriving programs, indicated by expansion of earlier offerings. These programs seem to have been set up with more forethought and planning than others that, according to responses, were not set up with much attention to specific needs.

Ninety-five percent of the respondents said that their program was developed to offer a well-rounded education. General marketable skills, such as computer skills, language skills, and management skills, were considered important, as opposed to focusing the program on one area, such as security or corrections.

Approximately 50% of the respondents indicated that their programs were professionally oriented, while the remainder reported that their programs had a liberal arts focus. Two programs indicated that their orientation was vocational.

Approximately 35% of the programs remain targeted toward criminal justice, and another 35% are interdisciplinary. Only 20% indicated that their programs are solely security oriented. The remainder reported that their programs offer a safety or business focus.

Experience of Faculty

Far too often courses are taught by people who have little or no practical experience in the field. Not only will students benefit more from someone who has field experience, but many times the students see this lack of real world exposure as a weakness in the teacher which may inhibit the learning process. The student should research faculty credentials. This can be accomplished by visiting the school and meeting with the faculty and asking for a biographical outline of all of the faculty from the department.

The programs responding to the survey reported a total of forty fulltime faculty members and fifty part-timers. That works out, on average, to one-to-two full-time faculty members for each program, with one-to-two part-time faculty assisting. We speculate that the part-time faculty is used to teach specialty courses while full-time staff members teach introductory courses, core classes, and those dealing with theory.

Of total faculty, twenty-three, or about 20 to 25%, were identified as being members of ASIS. Ten members, or a little less than 10% of the total faculty among the programs, were identified as having the CPP designation.

The backgrounds of faculty members are quite diverse. Since many of the programs were add-ons to existing criminal justice and law enforcement programs, 35% of the faculty teaching secufity courses report police backgrounds, with 20% having local or state public law enforcement experience, and 15% noting a federal law enforcement background.

As the above backgrounds reveal, approximately 70% of the faculty members teaching security do not have security backgrounds. Of those that do, the most frequently reported security specific background was industrial security, with the next frequent experience being in corporate security. Behind that were contract, hospital, and educational security backgrounds. Institutional security and retail were the least frequently reported background fields for security faculty. Another 15% have correctional and military backgrounds, which we consider security-related experience.

Consultants make up only 15% of the teaching staff. In other words, 85% of the faculty that teaches security is not involved in security consulting work.

While faculty may lack a background in private security, all the respondent programs indicated that they subscribed to *Security Management* and to the *Journal of Security Administration*. *Security* magazine was next in popularity.

Information on current students is lacking at most schools. Most programs surveyed did not keep accurate records on the number of full and part-time students they had nor were they able to report on the number of graduates at the graduate or baccalaureate levels. We are at a loss to explain the lack of record keeping. One would think that these numbers would be necessary to justify keeping a program or expanding it.

The absence of data may explain why the number of programs has been dwindling. One possible explanation is that these program have interdisciplinary degrees. If that is the case, records may be kept in other departments.

Of those reporting information, the following profile emerged: 70% of the students are male, and 80% are pre-service. Approximately 15% had prior experience but were not currently employed.

Of those who obtained employment after graduation approximately 30% found jobs in retail, 10% in public law enforcement, 10% with governmental programs and 10% with contract security firms. The remaining 30% were equally divided between industrial, institutional, hotel, military, correctional, consulting, educational, hospital, and corporate careers.

The Future

The future for security education programs is far from certain. Many of those who responded to our inquiry no longer offer programs. Those that do, mostly offer masters level work and intend to retain their prodivided programs. The respondents to whether or not the discipline is ready to support a Ph.D. in security administration or a related field was varied. The negative responses indicated that there was not enough support for such a program and that it was not an academic program with appropriate theoretical underpinings. The respondents were divided on whether or not they were going to be able to plan program-changes. Financial uncertainty, the needs of the security community, and control by other departments all appear to be key issues.

One of the problems with programs in security may be that many of the people who teach in this discipline have little or no experience of a practical nature in the field of security or loss prevention. Another factor relevant to the future of security programs is the use of advisory boards. As noted, the programs that are most successful have used advisory boards or committees. Input from experts and practitioners would seem imperative.

Given the amount of research related to education that was conducted by the Task Force on Private Security, as well as the early work of the ASIS Standing Committee on Academic Programs, security education should have succeeded. Unfortunately, the recommendations set forth were not incorporated into most programs.

Interdisciplinary programs are a must. Security managers operate first and foremost in a business environment that they must understand. They work with people more than with things. Security managers oversee.security operations and may become involved in law enforcement issues. All four areas are important. It does not matter which department houses the program, the program must allow students the opportunity to receive a well-rounded education.

References

Bottom, Norman R. Jr. <u>Research in Criminal Justice—The Private Security Connection</u>, paper presented at the annual meeting of the Midwest Association of Criminal Justice Educators, Moline, Illinios October 1979.

Cunningham, William C., John J. Strauchs, Clifford Van Meter, *The Hallcrest Report II: Private Security Trends 1970 - 2000*. Boston: Butterworth-Heinemann, 1990.

Parsons, Kevin, <u>Security Administration: Pseudo Science or Social Science Frontier?</u> paper presented at the annual meeint of the Midwest Association of Criminal Justice Educators, Moline, Illinois, October 1979.